BECOMING
WILD

ALAYNA COLE

BECOMING WILD

ALAYNA COLE

REVOLUTIONARIES
Gubbi Gubbi Country
Australia

ISBN 978-0-6459852-2-1

Editor
Wallea Eaglehawk

Copy editors
Sarah Bradbury
Emma Mitchell

Cover art and design by Cat McNicholl

First published in 2024

Revolutionaries
Gubbi Gubbi Country, Australia
www.revolutionaries.com.au

OTHER TITLES FROM THE AUTHOR

Queerly Ever After

CONTENTS

Content warning

These essays contain reference to many confronting topics, including:
- self harm and suicidal ideation
- eating disorders, weight, and body image
- discrimination, including queerphobia and ableism
- abuse and gaslighting

I encourage you to use your discretion if these are challenging topics for you.

INTRODUCTION

This is the most important time in human history. I don't mean to say today's date on the calendar is significant; rather, *now* is more important than everything that came before it and everything that comes after it. *Now*—the moment I am writing this, the moment you are reading it—is the only moment that we can tangibly influence, as individuals and as a society.

The past plays a role: we build upon (or ignore) our personal histories and humanity's learnings as we march onwards. The future is important, too: its endless potential inspires us to make better decisions now, for the sake of what's still to come. But as we navigate the fallacies of our memories, the biases in our written histories, and the anxieties of our future, nothing can be as *real* as now.

I genuinely believe that we live in the most interesting and wonderful period in history. Technology is evolving exponentially. We are more connected to our global neighbours than ever before, we are getting closer to being able to save human lives with transplanted organs from animals, and a telescope is currently sending us images of clouds from approximately 6,500 light years away from Earth.[1,2] Human rights are also arguably better than they have ever been as we constantly improve the depth of our education and knowledge, our understanding of medical treatments and hygiene, and the length of our lifespans (although this comes at the price of gender inequity, societal hierarchies, and environmental harm that were arguably not considerations of humanity's ancient ancestors).[3]

As a queer disabled woman, I have more social, economic, and political power in this moment than I would have had at any other time in recorded history. In Australia, women like me were only given the opportunity to vote for our federal political representatives in 1902 (although Indigenous Australians were made to wait until 1984 to receive equal elector rights).[4,5] I have fibromyalgia, a chronic pain condition that only gained medically recognised diagnostic criteria in 1990.[6] I could have been arrested for having a sexual relationship with another woman until 1997, when the last Australian state decriminalised homosexuality.[7]

Despite the unprecedented nature of this moment, however, history repeats itself. Amnesty International found in its 2022-23 report that human rights are being eroded globally, with increases in global conflict and war crimes, double standards of wealthy nations regarding issues like health care and refugees, and legislation impacting people's access to medical abortion or ability to seek gender reaffirming care.[8] The United States' annual report identified similar impacts to human rights and democracy, highlighting gender inequality in Afghanistan, religious genocide in China, and police violence against Black people in the United States itself.[9]

As human rights deteriorate and technology improves, people are seeking ways to find comfort and purpose. The tension between science and spirituality can be traced through centuries as humans continue to seek both answers and meaning. Desire to reconnect with nature resurges with each economic boom, and a hunger to improve ourselves and our prospects returns as we face global financial challenges.[10,11] Humans are always seeking something; that's why the self-help and wellness industries are thriving.

Self-help and wellness garnered an estimated global value of $US 41.[81] billion in 2021.[12] The success of the various books and products on the market may be due to their incredible effectiveness, but it's more likely a result of their marketing genius. These industries target the gnawing dissatisfaction they know is endemic in the Western world and deliberately cultivate guilt and shame in us, trying to convince us that we could—*and should*—be better versions of ourselves.[13] After pointing out the problem, they provide us with the solution: books and products designed to help us lose weight, be more productive, achieve career success, build stronger relationships, and find happiness.[11]

Self-help and wellness products aren't new. The first book that was specifically dedicated to the topic was published in 1859; its title, *Self-Help*, led to the name of the movement that continues today. Around the same time, better living products became popular. This selection of foods, tonics, and patent medicines were sold as ways to help us feel more alert, happier, or more fulfilled—which parallels how wellness products are marketed today.[14] Many well-known modern products started as better living products or patent medicines.

Coca-Cola was originally marketed as a health tonic, designed to help with mental acuity and nervous conditions—mostly due to the cocaine it contained until the early 1900s.[15] However, although this strategy can be found in old advertisements for Coca-Cola, the official Coca-Cola website denies it was ever marketed as a medicine; instead, it claims that, although it was first invented by a pharmacist and sold in a pharmacy, it was always a "soda fountain drink".[15]

Kellogg's cereal was also originally a wellness product.[16] The Kellogg brothers pioneered the idea of wellness at the Battle Creek Sanitarium, where controlled diets were part of the treatment plan for patients in the early 1900s.[17] Corn Flakes were first made as a breakfast solution that was convenient, nutritious, and helped treat the poor gastrointestinal health the brothers saw in their patients. Eventually, Will Keith Kellogg left the sanitarium to found the Battle Creek Toasted Corn Flake Company and mass-market their creation.[17]

As an aside, there's a myth that John Harvey Kellogg invented Corn Flakes to discourage masturbation because he considered it the "worst evil" a person could commit.[18] There's no clear evidence that was his motivation and it's more likely the brothers invented the cereal primarily as a digestive aid. However, there is evidence that John Harvey Kellogg was an avid eugenicist for the last 30 years of his life, so although he may have had a fantastic understanding of cereal, his understanding of evil was morally questionable.[19]

There's a reason the 1800s saw an increase in products targeting the health and wellbeing of individuals, while also encouraging people to treat their own ailments. Liberalism was on the rise in the mid-1800s and, for the first time, people—especially people in the middle and lower classes—were permitted to start thinking about themselves.[11] The working class was finally given the agency to control their own life and trajectory—and certain authors and inventors saw this as a marketing opportunity.

Since the 1800s, self-help and wellness has continued to evolve with the times, targeting the prevailing attitudes and needs of people in response to the historical context. During The Great Depression, the industry focused on teaching people how to attract money, become richer, and improve success in the job market.[11] After World War II, the focus shifted towards more spiritual approaches to self-help such as prayer and positive thinking. In the 1960s and 70s, people focused on unlocking their potential through new fitness trends and psychedelic drugs, with self-help and wellness products following suit.

The 1990s and 2000s saw a rise in self-help and wellness products that encouraged people to be optimistic and use the power of attraction.

The Secret was released in 2006 and became an international sensation, boosted by the support of Oprah Winfrey.[20,21] This same pervasive—and potentially dangerous—optimism led to the global financial crisis, and a new wave of derisive self-help (or anti-self-help) books followed.[11] *The Subtle Art of Not Giving a F*ck* has sold more than 10 million copies globally and holds its middle finger up to a lot of self-help rhetoric.[22,23]

If every period of self-help can be classified by a prevailing attitude, it seems like the current trend is cynicism. Heterosexual men seeking romance are turning to dating coaches and pick-up artists for advice and support—not out of a genuine desire to improve their ability to talk to women, but out of a sense of loathing for the women who have rejected them.[24] People are avoiding recommended medical treatments, not because of their support of alternative medicine but because of their distrust and dissatisfaction with conventional medicine.[25] We are often pushed to change our exercise routines because we should loathe our body shape or size, rather than being encouraged to revel in our bodies for the amazing things they are capable of doing.[26]

But is being motivated by hatred, dissatisfaction, and loathing really helping any of us?

I have always been prone to cynicism. I find it hard to trust others, I have limited faith in authority and institutions, and I can have a biting and dark sense of humour. My default approach to every situation is to find a sarcastic response or witty retort, rather than linger in a moment of sincerity. None of this is especially surprising, considering my age and cultural background: millennials are the most cynical of any generation, and Australians are known to be both self-deprecating and to mock others with our humour, supposedly to emphasise our informality and friendliness.[27,28]

Although I enjoy being unceremonious and cheeky, in the last couple of years, I've started to realise that instantly and habitually reaching for the joke can be a problem. We put people down for the activities they find beneficial or enjoyable, we deny our successes for the comfort of the people around us, and we close our door to friends who want to have sincere conversations about their feelings and challenges. We do all of this unintentionally by acting on autopilot, without thinking about the potential consequences.

I haven't given up my millennial cynicism or Australian sarcasm, but I've been using these responses more intentionally. Sometimes a conversation calls for a different approach and I'm trying to be more considerate of that before I speak, rather than instinctively reacting with a snarky joke. Although I am less likely to get an easy laugh, I've found that responding to people with kindness, compassion, and genuine interest can elicit surprising results.

Surrounding myself with people who are more interested in hyping each other up than tearing each other down has done more to improve my mental health than any self-help book I've read. Although the self-help industry promises it can improve our lives in myriad ways—wealth, love, friendships, admiration, beauty, health, or power— it tends to encourage us to look *inward* rather than outward.[13] Although we shouldn't be forced to sacrifice ourselves, our needs, and our wellbeing for the sake of others, we also need to be careful not to spend so much time thinking about self-help that it comes at the expense of the other relationships in our lives and our contribution to the communities we belong to.[29,13]

Studies suggest that we are becoming increasingly isolated from our communities. In 2019, a study found two in three millennials—people my age—felt disconnected from the people in their neighbourhoods and, of those, 57% were lonely.[30] Early studies into the effects of the COVID-19 pandemic have revealed that it has, on average, made us even lonelier—with lockdowns, social distancing, and remote work making us feel less connected to our peers.[31]

I live in Melbourne, where we faced one of the longest periods of COVID lockdown globally.[32] Between March 2020 and October 2021 we experienced six separate lockdown periods totalling more than 260 days. These lockdowns included rules restricting when we could leave the house, the radius we could travel, and the reasons we could go outside. While I am grateful for the protection this provided for my physical health, I spent eighteen months learning not to see people in-person, forgetting what activities I liked to do on the weekends, and unable to see smiles from behind masks. It was lonely.

As of mid-2023, our restrictions have all been lifted, more than 90% of Victorian adults have had at least one dose of COVID-19 vaccine, and case rates have become more manageable for our healthcare system.[33] However, I haven't re-learned the behaviours of my pre-pandemic life yet: I'm more likely to order food than to eat out at a restaurant, I tend to stream movies at home rather than go to the cinema, and I only travel to the office once or twice a week (despite living fifteen minutes away). This is partially due to new habits being difficult to break, but it's also a conscious choice; although some people are now acting as though the pandemic is over, early studies are showing that COVID-19 symptoms are exacerbated for people with fibromyalgia, so the risk of serious infection is higher for me than the average person.[34]

Vulnerable populations—including people from low socioeconomic areas, disabled people, and racial, ethnic, sexual, and gender minorities—are being disproportionately impacted by COVID-19, including the symptoms of the virus itself as well as the impacts that the pandemic has had on economic outcomes, education, housing, support structures, and access to medical care.[35] But early research suggests that COVID-19 could be considered a population-wide traumatic event— with mental health repercussions mirroring that of post-traumatic stress disorder—so even those who are promptly trying to return to normality may find themselves being significantly impacted by the repercussions of the pandemic for years to come without intervention and support.[36]

Feeling disconnected has notable health implications. Community bonds can make us happier, while loneliness is associated with a 30% increased risk of both heart attack and stroke.[30,37] Lack of social connections are as linked to negative health outcomes as smoking and can be more important than exercise.[37] Becoming involved in community initiatives like "volunteering ... attending religious services, joining a fitness group, or going to festivals" can reduce loneliness while also helping us solidify our sense of identity, improve our self-esteem, and lower stress.[37] The spaces away from our homes and our workplaces—also known as "third places"[38]—are sources of connection and community.

Third places were once plazas, markets, and theatres. More recently, they were bars, shopping malls, and libraries. But as we increasingly drink at home, shop online, and read from our tablets, we lose opportunities to meet others in spaces where social hierarchies are diminished—especially when coupled with the response to the pandemic.[39] Although digital spaces allow us to connect with people all over the world, there is something beneficial about meeting people in physical space who aren't chosen for us by an algorithm. Reconnecting with and reestablishing third places gives us an opportunity to build meaningful community with our neighbours, and being involved in something greater than ourselves helps us feel like we can make meaningful change in the lives of others, not just our own.

It can also be challenging to balance our attention between ourselves and others. Researchers have been studying the differences between selfishness and selflessness, and the impact that attitudes along this spectrum have on the economy, foreign aid, parenting, psychology and neuroscience, environmental conservation, culture, and more.[40-]

[45] Although examining population-level findings and turning them into individual solutions can be flawed, I still think this balance is something we struggle with both collectively and individually. It's something I've been working on in my own life for years.

Recently, I had the opportunity to participate in leadership training where I work. Sometimes, leadership training modules can feel like corporate-branded self-help, where a trainer recommends cookie cutter solutions designed to fix all of a company's problems after a half-day of reading from some out-dated slides. However, I am lucky to work for a company where our training feels less like corporate self-help and more like corporate *therapy*. There are some similarities between self-help and therapy, but therapy offers a few extra benefits: an individualised approach, encouragement to express yourself and connect learnings to your own experiences, a safe space without judgement, and opportunities to practise new techniques with the guidance of an expert.[46]

Many leadership training programs prioritise teaching management strategies and frameworks—theoretical ways of interpreting and interacting with the world. While we learned these too, before we talked about how we lead others, we were first asked to turn our gaze inwards and consider how we "lead the self". Just as our ability to help ourselves improves when we reconnect with our communities, our ability to work with others improves when we are better in-tune with ourselves and are able to hold ourselves accountable. Thus, the struggle between looking outwards and inwards is a false conflict: we cannot be happy, productive, and fulfilled unless we are actively doing *both*.

Bob Anderson, a researcher and leadership coach, summarises this idea perfectly:

> I believe we are here to contribute to the world—through developing our abilities to create results that matter—and also to become whole—by exploring and reframing our structure of beliefs. To combine these two efforts—to serve and to heal—is to be a leader.[47]

I first read these words between two of the leadership training modules I attended. They resonated with me so much that I wrote them out on a sticky-note and attached it to the wall beside my desk.

In the weeks before I stumbled across this quote, I'd been thinking about the concept of purpose more frequently, often in conjunction with musings about mortality and the potential legacy—however fleeting—that I'd like to leave behind one day. In the moment of clarity that struck me as I reached for my highlighter, I realised the reason I had not been able to determine my singular purpose up until then was that it is, in fact, twofold: to contribute to the world by serving others and to become whole by healing myself. Although I do not know for sure that this is the case for everybody— as Anderson confidently posits—it feels accurate for me.

Since understanding that my energy needs to be directed both inwards and outwards, I have started to recognise that, in my life, these efforts are cyclical. My motivation for spending time with others ebbs and flows, as does my enthusiasm for solitary and restful activities. Just as the leaves fall in autumn and we trust they will return in spring, I've been trying to avoid blaming myself for the ways my wants and needs change over time, trusting that I will be energised again when the clouds part and the Sun re-emerges.

For some people, this link between emotions and the weather is not just metaphorical. Seasonal affective disorder (or SAD, an acronym I imagine somebody is very proud to have created) refers to a condition where people experience moods that cycle with the seasons.[48] Most commonly, this condition involves people feeling less happy and motivated in the winter, with energy and enjoyment returning as the days become longer and warmer again.

However, I tend to find myself following the opposite pattern, becoming a social hermit around November—the end of spring in the southern hemisphere—and becoming energetic and lively again around February. I refer to this period as my "swamp witch" phase, where I metaphorically retreat into a tiny cottage in an isolated swamp like a fairytale witch, and I don't return until the humidity has subsided and my energy stores have been refilled.

Although seasonal affective disorder was first described by psychology researchers in 1984, it makes sense that people have been physically and emotionally responding to the seasons forever.[49] Our ability to survive has always been invariably tied to the natural cycles of the planet. For most of human history, the seasons have impacted our access to food, the day/night cycle directly influenced how many working hours we had in a day, and the phases of the Moon helped us track the passing of time. Many religions and spiritual beliefs form around these cycles and the ways they impact our lives—mine included. My own paganism stemmed from a desire to feel more connected to the world I inhabited, and to bring historical meaning to the traditions I once thoughtlessly followed. Pagan beliefs have been adopted and modified by other religious and secular societies throughout history, meaning many people now spend their year celebrating the birth of new life by exchanging Easter eggs or the harvest season by carving pumpkins, often without realising the significance of these commercialised rituals.

Despite the ways nature impacts us, studies have started to suggest that we're becoming more disconnected from nature.[50] Nature is becoming a less significant part of our collective imagination and cultural artefacts. Natural imagery has been declining in our music, books, and film since the 1950s, while references to human-made structures and environments remain steady.[50] Some theorise that urbanisation is the cause of this separation from nature, while others suggest it is specifically due to our recreational activities shifting indoors with the invention of television, videogames, and the internet.[51,52,50] Regardless of the cause, the result of people spending less time in nature remains the same.

Just as being isolated from our community can have negative consequences for our health, so can being disconnected from nature. Studies suggest spending time in natural environments can boost our attention, reduce stress, improve our mood, reduce our risk of psychiatric conditions, and even increase empathy and cooperation.[53] Researchers are starting to explore "forest therapy"[54] as a clinical treatment for depression. Non-fiction author and conservationist Richard Louv has posited that lack of time spent in nature is the cause of a range of behavioural and mental health issues in children, and would like this to be officially recognised as a condition called "nature-deficit disorder".[55]

While it may not be the case for everyone, making a deliberate effort to spend time in nature almost always helps improve my mood—even when at first I don't feel like getting up and going outside. I am most at peace when I'm in the warm sunshine or a cool rain shower, listening to a flowing river or crashing waves, looking at huge trees or tiny patches of moss, and having a conversation with every butterfly and bee that I notice as I walk.

Don't get me wrong, I don't think fresh air is a cure-all. I remember seeing a meme that circulated on social media a few years ago featuring a photo of a rainforest and a photo of a fluoxetine capsule—a selective serotonin reuptake inhibitor (SSRI) and a common form of antidepressant medication. The caption over the rainforest said "THIS IS AN ANTIDEPRESSANT" while the caption over the pill said "THIS IS SHIT". This is a wildly aggressive way to tell random strangers on the internet you think their scientifically tested and medically prescribed treatment for the chemical imbalance in their brain is ineffective.

I take sertraline—another variety of SSRI—

every day. It helps me avoid reacting as quickly, or irrationally, to stimuli as I might otherwise. It reduces physiological symptoms like headaches and jaw pain, and means that I can sleep without night terrors and panic attacks. Medication is an important part of some people's mental health journey, mine included.

Individuals can choose whether or not they want to use allopathic medicine for any number of legitimate reasons, including personal preference, potential side effects, ongoing visibility of symptoms, cost, and mistrust of the pharmaceutical industry.[56] However, some reasons people avoid medications are based on misunderstandings or misinformation. For example, some cite not wanting to consume chemicals as the reason they prefer "natural" alternatives to allopathic medications, which is the attitude underpinning the forests-are-antidepressants meme.[57]

The wellness industry is at least partially responsible for more widespread rejection of chemicals. Wellness blogs say things like "as an advocator for living toxin free, I always try to avoid using products containing chemicals"[58] and "we want to empower the community to make and execute chemical free choices".[59] What this fails to recognise is that everything is chemicals.[60]

You are chemicals. I am chemicals. This book is chemicals.

When somebody shares a meme on social media about going out into a forest and breathing fresh air, they are suggesting that you consume a combination of approximately 78% nitrogen, 21% oxygen, and 1% other gases, including water vapour, aromatics, and pollutants.[61] This barely differs from the chemical composition of the stale air that you might sometimes experience inside. (Inside air contains a slightly higher quantity of pollutants, CO_2 and microbial volatile organic compounds [MVOCs] which, coupled with increased humidity, can cause stuffiness and a musty smell.)[62] Basically, they're telling you that it's nice to go outside sometimes and breathe marginally different chemicals to the ones that are inside.

Sweeping statements about unnatural chemicals in our food, hygiene products, cleaning supplies, and medications demonstrate how far removed we have become from the sources of these substances. One article I read while researching this book contained an anecdote about a man who didn't want to take the antibiotics and painkillers that he was prescribed by his doctor because he "hate[s] eating chemicals".[63] I understand this instinct to some extent. An over-reliance on antibiotics can lead to antimicrobial resistance (meaning bacteria we used to be able to deal with globally evolves so that our medications become less effective against them). Additionally, using painkillers excessively can cause us to develop a drug tolerance where we need to use more of the same medication in future for comparable results.[64,65]

However, there's a difference between being mindful of our medication usage and dismissing all medications as unnatural chemicals we don't want to consume at all. We wouldn't have antibiotics without nature. Penicillin was the first variety of antibiotics ever discovered and it's made from a mould called *penicillium chrysogenum*.[66] Some of the most common painkillers we use today are derived from plants, such as morphine and codeine, which are alkaloids found in opium poppies.[67] Salicylic acid is a naturally occurring substance found in willow bark. Its pain relief properties were first recorded by Hippocrates in classical Greece, and a synthetic version of salicylic acid is used to make aspirin.[68]

Perhaps when we shift from talking about naturally occurring medicines to synthetic versions of their active ingredients, the "unnatural chemicals" descriptor begins to hold water. But these synthetic compounds are not inherently worse for the people consuming them, or for the environment. Mass producing medications allows us to help a larger percentage of the human population who have treatable illnesses, without exhausting the planet's natural resources.[69] In some cases, creating synthetic medications is also more ethical. For example, scientists are currently working on a lab-produced version of *limulus amebocyte lysate*, which is a compound vital for administering blood tests that is currently sourced from horseshoe crabs.[69] Creating chemically identical versions of useful compounds allows us to continue learning from nature and healing humanity without unsustainably sourcing materials from the plants and animals that have shared this knowledge with us. Even when medicines are unnatural, they are often inspired by nature or created in service of nature.

Sometimes it's tempting to see the world in black and white. It's easy to make sweeping statements like, "all allopathic medicines are unnatural and harm us", or "all alternative medicines are useless and unsupported by scientific evidence", but these extreme positions just aren't *true*.

In reality, it's all a lot more complex.

Complexity is scary—it's why people wax lyrical about returning to a simpler time. But that time doesn't really exist. Humans have always been complicated; we have spent our entire history trading one complexity for another. Medical treatment may have seemed simpler when we all relied on natural remedies, but treatments were also entirely unregulated and we collectively lacked huge swathes of knowledge. Germ theory has only been around for a couple of hundred years, viruses were only discovered in the 1890s, and hand-washing wasn't an official requirement for doctors in the United States until 1980.[70-72] While it was probably *simpler* for both doctors and patients when there were fewer documented illnesses to remember and hygiene was optional, it certainly wasn't more *effective*. There are economic and ethical issues that we need to navigate as we examine contemporary issues within our healthcare system—like health insurance, private ownership of pharmaceuticals, and lack of access to life-saving medical treatment in developing countries—but the solution isn't returning to a mythical simpler time. We need to commit to moving forwards together towards a better society.

My curiosity around the complicated ways that science and technology impact us—both individually and collectively—is what led me to many of the topics I explore in the essays comprising this book. As we retreat into comfortable urban environments, we become more socially isolated and disconnected from nature, which has demonstrable negative consequences on our health. The scientific method has brought us more effective and efficient healthcare, but it has also answered questions whose mysteries used to encourage storytelling and spirituality. We don't need to pray to Zeus now that we understand the physics of lightning storms— which is simultaneously a testament to humanity's growing knowledge and an unfortunate loss of our mythology.

The intersections between science and spirituality were the inspiration for many occult groups in the 19th and 20th centuries, where philosophers tried to integrate their esoteric interests with the scientific discoveries of the Modern era so they could justify embracing scientific progress without losing the enchantment of inexplicable phenomena.[73] Occultists gathered together and discussed magic, astrology, alchemy, the supernatural, and various forms of divination, as well as how these concepts could co-exist with recent scientific discoveries.[74] Many of these occult groups remain, in some form, today.

I believe in some of the ideas explored by the occult sciences, and I'm academically interested in others, but I still wouldn't consider myself an occultist. Occultism has been a playground for the political far right for decades, and occult groups have a tendency to perpetuate the heteropatriarchal power structures that marginalise anybody who is not an able-bodied, straight, white, cis man.[75] The Nazis were fascinated with the occult, and used divisions of psychics to help conduct military operations.[76] Contemporary right-wing political movements have aligned themselves with satanic ideologies and co-opted pagan symbols, and it's causing fractures within contemporary paganism.[77] Through this discourse, the political far-right has managed to infiltrate a significant number of neopagan groups and communities online. Thankfully, although the internet has guided my practice and fueled my research, my spirituality is found elsewhere.

Somehow in this introduction, we have already spoken about eugenics, human rights violations, the COVID-[19] pandemic, the looming threat to our mortality, and the challenge of managing our mental health. This perfectly captures both the way my brain constantly bounces from topic to topic, as well as my distinct inability to do small talk. If you're still with me, despite our immediate dabbling in stigmatised topics like politics, religion, and death, then *you* are my people.

I invite you to continue thinking about difficult topics and being vulnerable with me, as we challenge the expectations placed upon us by the spaces we inhabit. Scientific advancement, technology, and global connectivity has completely transformed what it means to be human—like sand that has melted into glass. We have been displaced from the natural world we once inhabited, instead becoming caged by the guilt and shame that we often feel for choosing to be *ourselves*. But just as glass can return to the ocean and be reshaped by the tides into something magical, we can choose to reconnect with the cycles of the Earth, rediscover our history, and reimagine ourselves.

When we are taught to think and behave in particular ways, it can feel rebellious—or *wild*—to pause, reflect, and dare to question that reality. But I've learned if I am going to find any semblance of balance in my life, I need to embrace that chaos.

These pages contain research and stories about witchcraft, marginalisation, diet culture, hysteria, phytochemistry, home appliances, tarot cards, herbal medicine, neurodivergence, chronic illness, and the Moon. Through these stories, I hope we can combat the effects of isolation and disconnection by seeking spirituality in the ceaseless determination, vulnerability, and compassion of people in our communities. It's time to question the narratives we have always been told that make us feel smaller than we are.

It's time to reclaim these stories and tell our own.

This is mine.

PAGANISM, WITCHCRAFT, AND HOWLING AT THE MOON

Humans have always had a natural tendency to look at the world around us and be stunned by the majesty of a colourful sunset, a towering tree, or a terrifying storm. The changing of the seasons and phases of the Moon continue to inspire poetry, paintings, and performances around the world. Until fairly recently, however, being in tune with these cycles was also a necessity for everyday life, and still is for some cultures. It's only been in recent decades that we have had access to technology that allows us to regulate temperature, buy fresh produce no matter the season, and access drinking water by turning on a tap.

Forms of spirituality focused on the sacredness of nature and natural cycles are often referred to as pagan. Pagan beliefs range from ancient traditions through to contemporary faiths, covering millennia of humankind's preoccupation with the natural world. We have returned to pagan beliefs again and again throughout history, unable to disentangle ourselves from the Earth on which we live.

In the 2021 Australian Census, I listed my religion as "pagan" for the first time on an official document. Throughout the years, I have identified as many different religions and spiritualities. As an infant, I was baptised Catholic and went to Catholic school for twelve years, but I always struggled with both the faith's core beliefs and the way the religious corporation operates. While I was at school, everything tended to feel like a distinct binary: you were academically-minded or a *bad student*; you were heterosexual or broken; you were Catholic or *didn't believe in anything*. (For anyone wondering, I was an academically-minded broken teenager who thought she was an atheist until she graduated.)

University offered new perspectives, and I remember learning the word pantheist over lunch one day on campus and changing my religion on Facebook immediately. Honestly, pantheism isn't altogether different from what I believe now: it's the belief that the divine is real, but instead of being personified by a god (or God), it's the universe in its entirety—including ourselves. Pantheism bestows every creature, every object, and every star with the same divine energy.

This can be interpreted as an abstract spiritual concept, but also as a more concrete scientific one. Astronomers like Harlow Shapley and Carl Sagan have been calling us "star stuff"[78,79] for decades, and a survey of 150,000 stars has shown that we share approximately 97% of their chemical make-up.[80] Whether that stardust is hydrogen or the holy spirit, it feels equally magical to me.

Nowadays, I identify as pagan, not a pantheist. There's no particularly articulate reason why.

Perhaps I prefer the groundedness of a faith that feels more focused on the dirt beneath my feet than the wide expanse of the universe, or I enjoy feeling connected to my ancestors, or I just want to feel like I've changed since the period of fervent self-discovery I went through as an undergraduate student.

Although paganism has existed for centuries, people only began to self-identify as pagan in the last hundred years.[81] The term pagan is derived from the Latin *paganus*, which means rustic or rural. When it first became common in the 5th century, it was a derogatory name for non-Christians, and was used interchangeably with words like hellene, gentile, and heathen. These terms propagated the idea that all non-Christian faiths—not just pre-Christian or religious spiritualities—were primitive or inferior, and worshipped false gods.

Due to the complicated history of paganism—as both a practice as a term—people observing contemporary forms of nature worship and polytheism have mixed feelings about calling themselves pagan. Some avoid the word entirely, while others see the label as a reclamation and wear it with pride.[82] I fall into the latter group; I find it poetic to proudly use a word that the faith I was raised in once used as a slur. (There are similar motivations behind my tendency to refer to myself as queer.)

Although I like the word pagan, I will admit it is a very *broad* term. While there are some underpinning similarities between pagan faiths, the term can refer to thousands of different practices across humanity's vast history and geography. To make studying these various forms of paganism more accessible, Ian Bonewits proposed three subsections of paganism: paleo-, meso-, and neopaganism.[83,84]

According to Bonewits' classification, paleopaganism describes early nature-based and polytheistic faiths that were unaffected by other religious and cultural forces. This is generally limited to pre- and non-Christian beliefs in and around Classical Europe (8th century BCE until 6th century CE), including Greco-Roman, Celtic, Germanic, and Slavic cultures. This includes Romuva, a pagan faith that was practised in the Lithuanian region and is still practised today.[85] (Although some scholars believe paleopagan should include other nature-based indigenous faiths from Asia, Africa, the Americas, and Oceania, this essentially colonises non-European faiths under a Christian European label without their consent.)[86]

Paleopagan practices found new followers during the Renaissance era (15th and 16th centuries) when Renaissance magic started being practised.[87] During this period, the lines were blurred between superstition, religion, scholarly knowledge, and occultism, with individuals turning to many sources to answer the questions science had yet to resolve. The seven *artes magicae*, or magical arts, referred to seven forms of divination that could be used to answer these questions: geomancy (using dirt or stone), hydromancy (using water), aeromancy (using sand or seeds tossed in the air), pyromancy (using a flame), necromancy (using blood or ritual sacrifice), chiromancy (using the lines on a person's palm), and scapulimancy (using the broken scapula of an animal).

The seventh of these magical arts feels *wildly* specific compared to the others, but interestingly scapulimancy has been practised all over the world, and was independently developed as a form of divination by people in Europe, Asia, and the Americas.[88] In this craft, the shoulder bone of an animal—usually sheep or ox in Europe and caribou, deer, or rabbit in North America—was heated over a flame until it cracked. The cracks were read to predict the future or determine which hunting paths would be most successful. Scapulimancy was a dominant form of magic during the Middle Ages and Renaissance in Europe, and was even mentioned by Chaucer in *Parson's Tale* in 1395.[89]

Interest in divination and the magical arts remained popular until the Disenchantment period of the 17th century as the increased fervour for witch trials made interest in the occult risky. However, paleopagan beliefs resurfaced again during the Romantic period ([18]th and 19th centuries) when nature-based traditions were reconstructed from fairytales as a reaction to the disconnection from nature that was occurring during the industrial revolution.[90],[91]

Bonewits' second category, mesopaganism, refers to faiths that combine paleopagan beliefs with monotheistic structures, like Christianity.[84] This includes many occult faiths, such as Freemasonry, Druidism, Theosophy, Crowley's Thelema, and Gardner's orthodox Wicca, all of which explicitly borrow from paleopagan practices, other religions, scientific knowledge, and each other.

Bonewits' final category, neopaganism, comprises

a diverse range of contemporary faiths that are continuations or revivals of paleopagan and mesopagan beliefs. In applying these traditions to a contemporary context, relevant political values and themes are often incorporated. This can range from feminist witchcraft movements that focus on gender liberation and social justice to right-wing Norse revivalists who celebrate their potential Viking lineage as a form of white supremacy.

Some neopagans—especially women—use the stereotypical witch as a symbol in their fight against inequity, resistance of the patriarchy, and search for community.[92] Considering my desire to reclaim terms like pagan and queer, perhaps it is unsurprising that I happily consider myself a witch. This form of neopaganism encourages women to be subversive, assertive, and supportive of each other. Mya Spalter, a writer and witch, believes her witchcraft is inherently political because, in a time where human rights are being eroded, it's "political to believe in the oneness of life on Earth".[92]

While the majority of neopagans have socially progressive beliefs, there are also pagans on the other end of the political spectrum.[93] Inspired by the writings of mesopagan occultists, right-wing extremists have created their own occult, satanist, or neopagan groups like the White Order of Thule and the Order of Nine Angles.[94,95] These groups also reclaim—or, more accurately, co-opt—symbols to disseminate their views. For example, one of the most significant images from the US Capitol attack on 6 January 2023 was of Jacob Chansley, a right-wing extremist with prominent Norse tattoos on his chest.[96] Symbols like Mjölnir (Thor's hammer),

Yggdrasill (the Tree of Life), and the valknut tattooed on Chansley's chest—as well as the Elder Futhark rune Othala and the Sun cross (which is often called the Celtic cross despite not being Celtic in origin)—have been adopted by white supremacists as a way of signalling their political alignment to each other.[97,98] Norse iconography has been deliberately chosen, as there is a pervasive myth that Viking culture was racially "pure".[99] This is not the first time white supremacists have taken ancient symbols and misappropriated them; the swastika was originally a Sanskrit symbol meaning good fortune or wellbeing. It has been found throughout ancient India, China, Africa, America, and Europe, but is now the most recognisable symbol of the Nazi regime.[100]

In response, other neopagans have formed groups like the Bristol-based nonprofit Heathens Against Hate to educate the public about the origins of pre-Christian symbols and the anti-discriminatory beliefs of many contemporary pagans. However, by stealing these icons and aligning themselves with ancient European paganism, white supremacists make it more difficult for socially progressive neopagans to associate with these beliefs and symbols without inadvertently suggesting they are allies to a discriminatory movement they don't agree with.

Political beliefs are not the only area of contention among contemporary pagans. Neopagan beliefs are vastly different between groups and although they share a common interest in nature, their similarities sometimes stop there. There are distinct differences between groups and their orthopraxy—whether they incorporate magic, which calendar and holidays they follow, whether they favour reconstructionist or eclectic traditions, and whether they follow a liberal or conservative approach to social issues (such as sexuality, gender roles, and restrictions on membership based on historical precedent).

Reconstructionist pagan faiths use pre-Christian, folkloric, and ethnographic sources to revive what they believe is a faithful reconstruction of an original paleopagan faith.[101] An example of a reconstructionist faith is Roman Polytheistic Reconstructionism, which attempts to revive ancient Roman paganism. Hellenism is similar, but instead reconstructs the beliefs and practices of ancient Greeks, specifically dedicated to the pantheon that was revered during the Hellenistic period between 323 BCE and 31 BCE. Heathenry reconstructs Germanic, Scandinavian, and Anglo-Saxon pre-Christian beliefs, while Celtic Reconstructionist Paganism focuses on Celtic traditions, and Slavic Native Faith (also known as Rodnovery) draws on traditional pagan systems of Central and Eastern Europe.

In contrast, followers of eclectic paganism understand that their beliefs are contemporary and, although inspired by various sources, do not try to practise historically accurate continuations of paleopagan faiths.[82] Eclectic paganism can be a unique and individual collection of beliefs that one person has constructed for their own spiritual journey, or it can describe the traditions of a larger pagan subgroup. For example, Neo-Druidism is an eclectic pagan faith based on the mesopagan

Druidic beliefs that were spread during the Romantic era and is inspired by Celtic history.

I understand the appeal of exploring ancient history. I'm fascinated by Celtic history too—primarily because I can trace a vast majority of my heritage back to Anglo-Saxon and Celtic ancestors from Scotland, Ireland, England, and Wales. When I first visited the United Kingdom in 2019, I remember stepping off the plane at Heathrow Airport and being struck by something beyond explanation. Perhaps it was just the jetlag, but I immediately felt like there was something significant about standing in that spot, like my feet had been craving that particular ground and my lungs had been wanting that particular air since I was born. As I explored London, I experienced a sensation similar to déjà vu on multiple occasions. It reminded me of going back to places I hadn't visited since I was a child; the specifics had changed and the scale of everything was wrong, but I knew I had been there before.

Before this experience, my paganism was a collection of disconnected interests without a name. I had collected pretty feathers, interesting stones, and good sticks since I was a child; I learned to use divination tools and draw labyrinths when I was a teenager; and I felt most at peace when surrounded by trees or listening to running water. But after I returned home, I started researching Celtic history and other paleopagan beliefs systems, and began to realise that these hobbies were more than ways to pass the time—they were my spirituality.

I learned that our contemporary understanding of the Celts—an Iron Age culture who lived in

Western Europe between 500 BCE and 500 CE—
is relatively limited.[102] Most historical records
about the Celts were written after Christianity
was dominant in the region, and Roman writing
deliberately depicted the Celts as uncivilised to
justify their conquering of them, a technique we
have seen used by colonising forces throughout
history.[103]

I'm inspired by the elements of Celtic history that
have been discovered, however, and by the critical
thinking we need to apply to make sense of these
discoveries. For example, records depicting Celtic
myths feature names that translate to meanings
like son of holly and daughter of yew, which
suggests the Celts venerated particular trees.[104] In
the 1st century, Stabo reported that oak groves were
considered sacred places where Celts met and Pliny
the Elder wrote about Druids climbing the boughs
of oak trees as part of a fertility rite.[105] Hazel wood
was used to make wands and divining rods, and
leaves and nuts from hazel trees have been found
in Irish and Welsh burial mounds.[106]

We can learn a lot about people from their burial
practices. I love visiting cemeteries, especially when
they are sprawling affairs with sections dedicated
to different faiths and cultures. Sometimes, I spend
days wandering through Fawkner Memorial Park,
the largest cemetery in Victoria. The bouquets of
flowers on Roman Catholic graves, the offerings of
mandarins and incense on Chinese burial sites, and
bottles of beer or flags from a favourite sports team
scattered through non-denominational sections.
But I was most struck by the stacks of stones and
glass beads on the Jewish graves. Stones are a

common Jewish offering when visiting a deceased loved one, potentially due to the traditional practice where stacks of stones were used to mark burial sites rather than headstones.[107,108] These stones can also act as a way to summon the soul of the departed so it stays with the visitor for the duration of their stay, as a token of respect that is more enduring than a bouquet of flowers, or as a marker to indicate to others somebody has visited to pay their respects.

This variety of offerings tells us as much about the person visiting as it does about the deceased (and their love of a particular beverage). This is why I love to wander cemeteries and try to understand the narratives being told through each vignette. It's also why archeologists have managed to make so many inferences about Celtic traditions and beliefs from their burial sites. For example, evidence of shrines or offerings have been found in locations near large rocks, forks in streams, the base of mountains, or important trees, demonstrating a potential Celtic fascination with nature.[109] Archeologists have also discovered food, weapons, and ornaments at burial sites, suggesting that Celts believed in some sort of afterlife where these items might be useful to their loved ones.[110] Other archeological discoveries of Celtic relics have included humanoid figures made from stone, carvings of animals and birds, and coins that copy Greek and Roman currency but featuring unique iconography like heads, horses, and the spiral and knot patterns we associate with the Celts today.[111,112]

Although archeologists and historians have attempted to make inferences about the contextless items and unreliable records they have found, there is no comprehensive and factual summary of the beliefs and traditions that Celtic people followed during the Iron Age. Similar can be said about faithfully recreating most paleopagan faiths. As a result, it's nearly impossible for reconstructionists to accurately create a belief system they can follow without filling gaps with modern interpretations or borrowed traditions.

However, eclectic faiths can be equally challenging. Although eclectic pagans are able to close gaps in their chosen spiritual practice by borrowing rituals and traditions from other faiths, this bowerbirding approach can lead to cultural appropriation if it isn't done with adequate research into closed practices and tokenism. I recently attended a local witches' market where many of the stalls were dedicated to the items pagans, druids, and nature practitioners use in our faith: gemstones, candles, jewellery, oracle cards, and other trinkets. It is common for stalls at these markets to sell items that belong to closed or culturally significant practices such as white sage, palo santo, dream catchers, and calaveras (sugar skulls).[113-116] These sellers rarely include information about the significance of these items or the environmental impacts of their popularity, instead providing them to the public for their aesthetic value or otherwise expecting market goers to do the research themselves.

And that research can be difficult. Searching for information about closed practices takes you into forums where practitioners argue whether or not they should be allowed to use items that have cultural significance for groups they aren't from and, if so, in which situations. For example, the majority of Mexican people are happy that people want to engage with the traditions of Día de los Muertos and only have a problem if calaveras are used as symbols or costumes during Halloween; however, this isn't the perspective of *every* Mexican person so it can be difficult to decide which advice to follow.[116]

As another example, some practitioners argue people should be allowed to use white sage and palo santo because they come from the Earth, and that it's specific rituals like smudging that are closed practices. Regardless of these semantics, the enthusiastic use of these plants by witches and the wellness industry globally has created a market that major chain stores have seized. Palo santo trees are being cut down prematurely (and illegally) before they have time to form their spiritually significant resin.[114] White sage is also harvested in ways that are "rushed and violent" rather than being hand-gathered and prayed over.[113] Although white sage and palo santo are not currently considered endangered, they are being grown more on private land and in monoculture plantations, which threatens the natural habitats that these plants would normally grow in, as well as the animals and other plants that rely on those ecosystems.[114] This also leads to reduced access to these natural resources for the people for whom they are sacred.[113] Does any eclectic pagan need access to these particular plants so badly that they would risk the conservation of ecosystems and the preservation of Indigenous cultures that colonists have attempted to suppress and assimilate for decades?

One well-known eclectic pagan faith that has struggled with cultural appropriation is Wicca. The term Wicca refers to a range of practices, from the traditional beliefs originally created by Gerald Gardner—an occultist and self-proclaimed witch who is considered the Father of Wicca— to contemporary interpretations that focus on witchcraft, nature, and social justice to varying degrees. There has been debate about whether the term should only be used to describe the faith when it strictly adheres to the rules originally proclaimed by Gardner (known as British Traditional Wicca or Gardnerian Wicca), or if the term can also be used to describe a broader and more inclusive faith.[117] Doreen Valiente, who was involved in creating the original Wiccan texts with Gardner, argued for a more inclusive Wicca throughout her life.[117]

Although the term Wicca is derived from the same Old English etymological root as the word witch, the two words aren't interchangeable; not all people who practise Wicca would describe themselves as witches, and many spiritual witches do not ascribe to a Wiccan tradition. I refer to myself as a pagan or witch, but never Wiccan. The primary reason for that is the Father of Wicca himself, who is a problematic figure and an indelible part of the faith.

But to understand my issues with Gardner, we first need to explore his earlier life and the interests he pursued before he founded his own faith. Gardner spent much of his life travelling abroad, and was fascinated by the diverse beliefs and magical practices of the cultures he encountered. When he returned to England in the late 1930s, he dabbled in various occult groups alongside the founders of many mesopagan faiths.

Occultist gatherings were a popular esoteric pastime for scholars and philosophers in the 19th and 20th centuries. The term occult, however, has been used since the 16th century, where the occult sciences described areas outside the realm of science and religion, such as astrology, alchemy, magic, and the supernatural. Occultism, as a separate term, first appeared in France and was introduced to English by Helena Blavatsky in 1875.[118,119] Practices like spiritualism, theosophy, and anthroposophy are considered occult, as well as organisations like the Freemasons and the Hermetic Order of the Golden Dawn.

The etymology of occult is surprisingly interesting. When I started researching the term, I imagined it would share a common root with the word cult—after all, both terms are used to describe belief systems that are often esoteric, New Age, or pseudo-religious. However, I was surprised to learn that although both words are derived from Latin, their roots are different. Occult comes from the joining of the prefix *ob* (as in obstruct and obfuscate) and the root *celare* (to hide or conceal), referring to the secretive nature of occult groups. Meanwhile, cult comes from *colere* (farming and worship)—the same root that developed into words like cultivate (tend to land or develop a skill) and culture (developing a group through shared education and artistic pursuits)—referring instead to the intentional and ritualistic nature of cult practices. I also found it interesting—although even more tangential—to discover that the term occult has no meaningful relationship to the word ocular. Considering ocular refers to the eyes and vision, I thought it might be related to a root word about concealment, but ocular actually comes via French from the Latin root *oculus* (meaning eye). That's why occult has two Cs and ocular only has one. Although the relationship between the words occult, cult, and ocular is coincidental, it's possible that these terms had more staying power in English than alternatives due to their apparent similarities.

Just as these terms seem to have staying power, so too do the concepts that they represent. The Enlightenment of the 17th and 18th centuries answered many of the questions that had historically been addressed through religion and magic. However, despite its ability to give definitive answers to previously unknown phenomena, science left many people feeling a sense of loss.[120] There was a collective feeling of disenchantment, which led to occultism resurging in the 18th and 19th centuries. This resurgence saw a shift away from the original occult sciences towards new forms of occultism, as occultists attempted to adapt traditional esotericism for the new world, allowing esotericism to exist alongside empirical scientific discovery.

Through his involvement in this occult movement, Gerald Gardner claims to have met members of the New Forest Coven, a secret organisation of witches who supposedly gathered in the New Forest region of the United Kingdom and dedicated themselves to maintaining and passing down the traditions of the Witch-Cult.

The Witch-Cult hypothesis claims witches who were persecuted during the Middle Ages practised a specific set of pre-Christian pagan traditions that could be considered witchcraft. The theory was first proposed by Professor Karl Ernest Jarcke in 1828, and became popular when Margaret Murray, a notable Egyptologist and occultist, included references to it in the witchcraft section of Encyclopaedia Britannica's 1929 edition. Although Murray's peers considered the Witch-Cult theory to be incorrect and based on false research, her section in the trusted Encyclopaedia Britannica was reprinted for decades, making her claims more influential than the work of other academics specialising in the witch trials who have proven the trials were actually caused by a combination of social, economic, and religious factors.[121-124]

Gardner met Murray through the Folklore Society, of which they were both members. Supposedly, Gardner was the only member of the society at the time who believed Murray's Witch-Cult theory.[125] This makes it particularly convenient that he then discovered the New Forest Coven, was initiated by its leaders, and invited to share their secret traditions with the world.

This tale is more common than you might think. For example, a relatively well-known modern spiritualist and author of oracle card decks, Travis McHenry, tells a similar story. McHenry claims to have been studying the dark arts in the late 1990s when he "stumbled upon a secretive coven of witches who subsequently befriended him and allowed him to publish the first written history of their magical tradition".[126] This text is taken from his author biography, and is almost an exact replica of Gardner's story.

Some scholars have claimed the New Forest coven was a fictional creation of Gardner, designed to give credibility to Murray's Witch-Cult theory as well as establish an historical basis for the new faith he was developing.[127-129] Others have suggested that a number of practitioners who shared an interest in the fiction of the Witch-Cult did gather informally in the New Forest area, creating a set of traditions based on these stories.[130] Either way, Gardner's claims that this coven read from texts originally created by pre-Christian witches is likely an attempt to establish a significant and reputable fictional history for his new faith thereby making it harder for historians to trace its true lineage—a common practice when occultists shared their beliefs. Presumably, it's for the same reason Murray referred to Gardner as a doctor in her writings about him and his faith, despite him not being one.[131]

Even if the New Forest Coven did exist in some form and did initiate Gardner in 1939 as he claims, there are debates about who exactly initiated him. Gardner suggested the leader of the coven was a woman named Dorothy Clutterbuck (who he referred to as Old Dorothy in his publications), but this could be a local joke due to Clutterbuck's prominence in the area at the time. Although Doreen Valiente also insists Clutterbuck was the leader of the coven, her involvement seems unlikely. Clutterbuck was a devoted Christian woman who was in mourning during the period Gardner claims to have been initiated, at which time she cancelled all social engagements.[128-130]

However, one scholar who believes Clutterbuck was in the New Forest coven is Philip Heselton, who suggests the nature poetry in Clutterbuck's diaries are proof of her pagan beliefs.[130] Her diaries—or commonplace books—contained poetry and illustrations that were more often focused on her spiritual connection to nature than Christianity. However, there's no definitive proof within them that Clutterbuck was a witch or a member of the New Forest coven, much less its leader.

As a brief aside, I had not heard of commonplace books until I started researching Dorothy Clutterbuck's diaries. Commonplace books are a type of notebook or scrapbook used to compile information such as proverbs, poems, quotes, letters, recipes, and lessons, often displayed somewhere prominent and designed to be shared with visitors to the home. They generally use subject headings to collate notes in sections for easy referencing, similar to a database.[132] Many notable historical figures used commonplace books to organise their research and thoughts, including Isaac Newton, Virginia Woolf, Ronald Reagan, and H.P. Lovecraft.[132] In some ways, this collection of essays is akin to a modern commonplace book: a unique text compiling research about topics that interest me, accompanied by my responses and thoughts.

If Clutterbuck's commonplace books are not evidence of her involvement in the New Forest Coven, then who else might have initiated Gardner?

Some scholars who believe in the existence of the coven have suggested Edith Rose Woodford-Grimes (better known in pagan circles as Dafo) helped Gardner establish his new faith. Regardless of whether Dafo was a member of the mythical New Forest coven, she *did* help Gardner write his Book of Shadows, which became the foundational text for the rituals and traditions still used in British Traditional Wicca. Gardner claimed his Book of Shadows collated the "fragmentary"[129] practices of the New Forest coven and preserved the traditions of the Witch-Cult while simultaneously filling gaps in their ceremonies and beliefs with an eclectic mix of practices, which he borrowed from other occult groups and shamelessly appropriated from other cultures that he observed during his travels earlier in his life.[129]

As the popularity of Wicca grew—and, subsequently, Gardner's desire for publicity—Dafo decided to step away from the faith due to the risk of her true identity being exposed.[133] At that time, her involvement in witchcraft was a secret she kept from her family and her identity as Woodford-Grimes was only publicly revealed in the late 1990s.

Before she left, Dafo met with Doreen Valiente on several occasions and, on the summer solstice in 1953, Gardner initiated Valiente into Wicca at Dafo's house.[133] Valiente became a High Priestess and a significant contributor to Wicca, acting as Gardner's business partner in Dafo's stead. Valiente wrote much of the best-known poetry found in Gardner's Book of Shadows, including the poem 'Charge of the Goddess', which has since been published separately.[134]

Gardner's Book of Shadows was a constantly evolving text. Throughout his life, Gardner added to and adapted the Book with new rules, rituals, and traditions that he gathered from a range of sources. He also frequently broke or changed his own rules, such as reducing the traditional one year and one day period that needed to pass between when a person begins studying Wicca and when they could be officially initiated.

Just as his Book of Shadows was a living document, Gardner encouraged others to create similar texts for their own practice. He revealed his Book of Shadows to initiates of Wicca, who would then copy down its contents, making changes to personalise the book for themselves. While more inclusive forms of Wicca still encourage similar experimentation and evolution, British Traditional Wicca prints identical copies of Gardner's Book of Shadows for its initiates to use, based on the copy that a High Priestess named Monique Wilson transcribed from Gardner's original book.

One of the changes Gardner made to his own Book of Shadows was to create a set of Wiccan Craft Laws. When the same publicity-seeking behaviours that originally drove Dafo away from Wicca began to cause a rift between Gardner and Valiente, Valiente proposed the 'Rules of the Craft' to Gardner, which she wrote in an attempt to curtail his obsession with public attention.[130] Gardner responded by stating the rules were unnecessary because Wicca already had a set of Laws; these Laws, which had conveniently not been seen before, explicitly limited the power of the High Priestess. In addition, Gardner's Laws stated that "the greatest virtue of a High Priestess be that She recognizes that youth is necessary to the representation of the Goddess" and that she should "gracefully retire in favor of a younger woman".[131] When Valiente learnt Gardner had only written his Craft Laws in response to her proposed rules, the original coven split.[133,117]

This was not the first evidence of Gardner's underlying misogyny. Wicca proclaims to be a welcoming and inclusive faith, with women adopting leadership roles within the hierarchy, participants donning flowing robes that disguise their gender, and many rituals exploring the masculine and feminine energies we all possess however, many of Gardner's traditions betray his desire to retain patriarchal structures.[135] For example, Gardner required all Wiccan initiates to have a lineage of initiation that directly traced back to him, and his Book of Shadows contains rules about women needing to be taught rites by men (which Valiente disagreed with). The Book of Shadows also contains "sex magic" and rituals involving nudity that are focused on women's bodies and virginity.[136]

One such ritual was known as the Great Rite, where the High Priest and High Priestess—representing the Horned God and Triple Goddess—would perform sexual acts to demonstrate the physical and metaphorical union between these opposing forces.[131,137] Although the acts themselves are said to be performed in private rather than in front of other ritual participants, it still demonstrates the sexism of the Laws that insist the High Priestess should be a younger woman while

Gardner was able to retain his status of High Priest for as long as he pleased.[135]

Gardner's Book of Shadows spoke openly about sex in other ways too. He described Skyclad rituals as practices that were performed while naked, to supposedly improve the flow of energy between your body and nature. He also spoke about sex as a spiritual act and described the ways it could influence magic. Gardner's claim that he did not write the foundational rituals of Wicca—rather, he simply transcribed the traditions of the New Forest coven—allowed him to forfeit responsibility for asking his followers to participate in these acts. Although these sexual practices in and of themselves are not necessarily predatory, encouraging them can create opportunities for predators to take advantage of individuals seeking spiritual enlightenment.[137]

Gavin and Yvonne Frost brought Wiccan ideas to the United States in 1969 when they started their School and Church of Wicca. They gave lectures, ran workshops, and authored books until Gavin died in 2016. In their book *The Witch's Bible*, the Frosts describe a rite where initiates who have "the physical attributes of reproduction"[138] (i.e. have reached puberty) are assigned an older sponsor of the opposite sex. Sponsors teach their initiates sexual techniques, with women being given wooden phalluses to practise with. Prior to the rite, the initiate and sponsor fast, drink mead, and dance naked, and then have penetrative sexual intercourse. In this chapter, the Frosts are actively encouraging the sexual assault and exploitation of minors in the name of Wicca.[137]

The Frosts were significant Wiccan leaders in the United States, but their interpretation is only one version of contemporary Wicca. After Gardner's death in the 1960s, leaders within Wicca fought over the appropriate way forward, causing Wicca to become fractured into various forms. For example, WITCH was a new age movement that began in the late 1960s that used Wicca to promote militant feminist ideas. WITCH allowed members to self-identify as a witch or Wiccan without needing to be indoctrinated by an existing member, which enraged traditional Wiccans. Other women's rights activists also evolved Wicca, expanding its focus on gender equality and sex positivity.

Women have always been drawn to Wicca, despite the influence of Gerald Gardner. Modern witchcraft is more focused on women than many other forms of neopaganism; although all genders are welcome to practise Wicca, modern evolutions of the faith tend to centre women's experiences and social justice more than other neopagan traditions like Druidism, Egyptian reconstructionism, and occultism.[139] Margot Adler was one of these practitioners; she wrote about Wicca as a social justice and environmentalist religion due to its respect for nature.[101] Laurie Cabot was another, who owned a witchcraft supply shop in Salem, Massachusetts, and wanted to bring public attention to witchcraft as a spiritual movement.[140]

At the forefront of the feminist revitalisation of Wicca was Doreen Valiente. While Gardner started Wicca with his book *Witchcraft Today* in 1954, Valiente marked its evolution in 1993 with her aptly named *Witchcraft for Tomorrow*.

Despite these attempts to reclaim Wiccan tradition and position it firmly in a contemporary feminist space, I still don't consider myself a Wiccan. I find the term Wicca is still too connected to Gardnerian assumptions that I prefer to avoid associating myself with. That said, I do follow some practices popularised by the Wiccan tradition, which makes sense considering the motivations that led to the formation of Wicca, and the similar forces that drive my own spirituality. When the routines of our lives begin to limit how often we find ourselves outside—such as careers that involve spending our days inside factories or offices— we are drawn towards rituals that encourage us to commune with nature more deliberately.[141] Traditions that reduce the barriers between myself and the natural world help me reconnect with the wild, liberated creature that exists within me.

One Wiccan tradition that I practise is celebrating the eight sabbats, a series of annual reminders to engage with the natural cycles of the Earth and the way our bodies inhabit them. These sabbats comprise a calendar called the Wheel of the Year, and includes Samhain, Yule, Imbolc, Ostara, Beltane, Litha, Lugnasadh, and Mabon. Some of these names might sound familiar—especially Yule, which is still used to describe various Christmas celebrations globally. Many of the Wheel of the Year celebrations have a parallel to Christian or secular observances, with similarities in how they are celebrated such as Samhain with Halloween, Ostara with Easter, and Mabon with Thanksgiving.

This isn't a coincidence; many of these well-known celebrations evolved from pagan and other global traditions, but these connections have become lost for most people who observe them. Some Wheel of the Year traditions can be traced back to the Middle Ages, like the maypole used for Beltane.[142] Even the titles of the observances have pagan roots, with the solstice and equinox names being derived from Germanic paganism, while the names of the other four festivals are derived from Celtic terms.[143]

The Wheel of the Year celebrations are evenly spaced throughout the calendar year, timed to the solstices (longest and shortest days), equinoxes (midpoints between the solstices), and approximately halfway between these days. Litha and Yule mark midsummer and midwinter respectively, and, on a traditional European pagan calendar, Yule aligns approximately with Christmas. But that doesn't make sense in the southern hemisphere. At Yule, we bring an evergreen into our homes to reconnect with a dormant earth and we give gifts to each other to help us get through the long nights. But, we do it in the middle of summer when the trees are covered in leaves and the days are delightfully full. Our traditions lose their meaning as we repeat the behaviours we have been told are associated with a celebration without understanding why, and we become disconnected from nature in the process.

While I am hearing about my friends and colleagues cramming themselves into crowded shopping centres and buying last-minute Christmas presents for their loved ones, I celebrate Litha. I spend time in the Sun, I share meals with friends, and I give loved ones gifts of lavender and chamomile to help them sleep when the nights become hot and restless. I save my Yuletide celebrations for Winter, when the nights are so cold and long that it feels like maybe the Sun will never rise again. I bake bread and make lanterns, and they keep me company through the darkness while I stay awake watching for the sunrise, just to make sure it returns.

Delicious meals are a commonality between many pagan festivals, whether it be partaking in the first bounty of a harvest or indulging in one last feast before the seasons change and the availability of certain foods changes with them. The Sun is also a common trend between the sabbats: spending time outside in it, lighting candles to remember it, or expressing gratitude to it. The Sun has been a companion to every person and creature who has ever existed on Earth: the life-bringer who grants us light, warmth, and energy. I have the Sun tattooed on my right hand, representing productivity, motivation, and action.

Celebrating the Sun during sabbats is one practice I've adopted from Wicca, and celebrating the Moon through her cycles is another. I've always been enamoured by the beauty of the Moon, especially when she's bright and full in the sky, and I enjoy watching her shape change throughout each month as a reminder of time passing. To counter the energy of the Sun, I have the Moon tattooed on my left hand, reminding me to pause, dream, and create. While I feel the warmth of the Sun in my mind, I feel the light of the Moon in my heart. The Sun is my companion while I work, but the Moon has been loyal during my late night adventures and early morning anxieties. We speak to the Sun, but we howl at the Moon.

People have always been fascinated by the Moon. The different phases of the Moon's cycle have been associated with many things throughout history, including emotions, travel, protection, wisdom, and yearning.[144] With the Moon acting as an important symbol, each full moon has also been given names by different cultures. It's well-documented that several Native American language groups named each full moon, as they were an important form of timekeeping and managing the seasons.[145] Although different tribes had variations on their names, there is a version that became standardised by colonial Americans, and has since spread further across the Northern Hemisphere. In this set of names, the first full moon of each month receives a unique title: January is Wolf, February is Snow, March is Worm, April is Pink, May is Flower, June is Strawberry, July is Buck, August is Sturgeon, September is Corn, October is Hunter, November is Beaver, and December is Cold.

Although I loved the idea of naming the full moons, these common names didn't make any sense for me; they had been created based on an intimate understanding of the seasons, climate, and ecosystems of North America. In Australia, we don't get snow in February, many of our flowers aren't blooming in May, and we don't harvest corn in September. We don't even *have* beavers. I couldn't just shift this set of names by six months like I did with the Wheel of the Year; I had to create my own names from scratch.

The first time I did this, I lived in Queensland

and used two decades of childhood experiences to inform the names I chose. After moving to Victoria, my first year in a new temperate climate made me realise that even within the same hemisphere—and the same country—the names no longer applied. The summers where I grew up were wet and stormy, but now winter is my rainy season. The turtles hatch and the whales pass the coast at different times of year here. It helped me feel more connected to the new environment as I paid attention to nature, and learned how it acts throughout the year in this new location, and it helped me feel more at home.

January became the Fire Moon because of the bushfires that are common in my region every summer. February is the Harvest Moon because I associate this month with gathering fruit and vegetables from the garden as the summer begins to cool. March is the Dry Moon because it's historically the driest month in Victoria, April is the Citrus Moon as the citrus trees begin to bear fruit, and May is the Whale Moon because it's when whales are most likely to be spotted off the coast nearest to where I live. June is the Cold Moon, as temperatures reach their lowest and the days become short. July is the Thunder Moon, as this month has the highest recorded rainfall where I live, and then August is the Floral Moon as those wet weeks and slightly warmer temperatures encourage the first spring flowers to start blooming. September is the Worm Moon, as the Earth reawakens and the natural cycles of growth begin again. October is the Magpie Moon, as the birds begin to nest and swooping season in Australia starts in earnest, with magpies diving towards passersby in an effort to protect their young. November is the Turtle Moon, with turtle eggs hatching on the beaches near me. And, finally, December is the Peach Moon, as stone fruit becomes ready for harvest and I can go to the local orchard to celebrate the start of summer.

There are thirteen full moons per year and only twelve months, so inevitably one month will have two full moons; this second moon is known as a blue moon (which is where the saying "once in a blue moon" originates). When you use that saying, you are literally saying "once per year". The names I chose for the remaining twelve moons are significant to me because of where I live and because of what I value. They highlight key parts of the annual natural cycle, celebrate the passing of time, and act as a reminder to engage with the earth in different ways throughout the year.

The act of naming the moons represents the reason I'm drawn to paganism: I adore the ways it finds magic in the mundane. Cycles like the changing of the seasons and migration of animals are significant to me—not because they're caused by sorcery, but precisely because they're *not*.

I've incorporated other tools and practises into my faith for similar reasons. For example, I am fascinated by the way people have taken the tarot cards that were originally used to play a gambling game in Europe and have turned it into a way to talk to each other about our futures, our intentions, and our traumas. I use tarot cards regularly when navigating challenges or seeking focus, not because I believe they innately contain the magical energy of an ancient people capable of telling my future, but rather because I know the guidance I need is inside me already, waiting to be spoken aloud.

Occultists approach their craft in completely the opposite way, manipulating the origins of activities and artefacts that they deem too mundane for the sake of creating a sense of mystery.[146] Ironically, by creating false mysteries around mundane items, occultists have created some actual mysteries in the origin stories of various magical practices, because their differing accounts have made tracing authentic historical lineage more challenging. According to some occultists, tarot cards have a storied history of fortune-telling dating back as far as 3100 BCE, with the figures that comprise the deck being modified from hieroglyphs. One contemporary university website states, in a blog post, that tarot cards were originally a book of knowledge "invented by the Ancients", [147] claiming it was disguised as a game so it could be used for fortune-telling without persecution for millennia. This same blog post suggests that perhaps ancient Egypt "is more ancient than we think",[147] and that ancient Egyptians were responsible for protecting "the wisdom and knowledge of Atlantis".[147]

Alternatively, Helena Blavatsky, a 19th century occultist, claimed the figures found on tarot cards (like the Hanged Man and the Magician) originated on "the Babylonian cylinders".[148] Some contemporary websites have tried to prove this assertion by sharing side-by-side images of Babylonian cylinder seals alongside drawings of tarot cards. (I can slightly see the resemblance if I squint my eyes and, in some cases, literally stand on my head.) Blavatsky goes beyond sharing her conspiracies about tarot's origins, additionally criticising anybody who is unaware of her proposed history. In *The Secret Doctrine*, Blavatsky gives a fierce burn to European fortune-tellers by claiming that the majority who used tarot cards to make their living were "sad specimens of failures of attempts at reading, let alone correctly interpreting, the symbolism of the Tarot".[148]

Associating ancient Egyptian and Babylonian iconography with the tarot is factually inaccurate, and exoticises ancient cultural practices.[146] Egyptian hieroglyphs and Babylonian seals are incredible glimpses into the long history of humanity, and claiming European traditions are connected to those ancient cultures simply because they are aesthetically appealing is akin to the more contemporary examples of cultural appropriation and orientalism.

Orientalism describes the way Western media presents Eastern cultures and history as "timeless and exotic"[149,150] because of the stereotypes created by 19th century Western art when it depicted Eastern regions as homogenous and exotic.[151] Ancient civilizations in Egypt and Babylon (which was situated in the area we now call Iraq) were simplified and reduced to their aesthetic appeal, which occultists chose to associate with to make their practices seem more mysterious.[151]

Realistically, if tarot had originated in Egypt or Iraq, then some historical traces of tarot would have been found in south-west Asia or north Africa, no matter how well practitioners hid their fortune-telling to avoid persecution. In addition, we would see evidence of the migration of tarot to Italy, where the oldest surviving tarot decks and references to games using tarot cards have been found.[146] However, there is no evidence of tarot cards appearing in south-west Asia, north Africa, or Greece and surrounding countries until the 20th century.[146]

So, what is the actual origin of tarot? It seems tarot cards—with their recognisable suits, their extra court cards, and depictions of figures like Death and Justice on trump cards—most likely originated in northern Italy in the early 1400s.[146] Evidence suggests the deck was originally only used for playing card games that involved trick-taking and ranking cards numerically based on their suits (swords, batons, cups, and coins). These games were based on other pastimes that were likely invented in China during the Tang dynasty, where cards were printed using woodblocks and distributed.[152] From here, similar cards can be traced through Persia and Arabia, into Egypt (although the fragments of cards found in Egypt are from the 12th and 13th century, not 3100 BC), and up into Europe.[153]

Playing cards, and the games that could be played with them, evolved constantly as they moved from place to place over several centuries. The invention of the tarot deck is attributed to the addition of 21 triumph cards, which occurred in Italy between 1440 and 1450, and featured illustrations of people like The Emperor, and concepts like The Chariot. These cards—shortened to trump cards—became a staple of the Italian *tarocchini* deck, the Austrian *konigrufen* deck, and the French *tarot* deck. There was also an expanded deck in Florence called the *minchiate*, which had a set of trump cards that included concepts like the astrological symbols and the four elements.[154]

Trump cards are known to contemporary cartomancers as the Major Arcana. Although the iconography on these cards were originally the same throughout most of Italy, their numerical values differed depending on where you travelled. The deck, and the games you could play with it, diversified even further as they travelled into France, Switzerland, Denmark, Austria, Hungary, Czechia, Slovenia, the former Ottoman Empire, and so on.[146]

The evolution of tarot from a playing card deck to a divination tool appears to have occurred in the late 1700s. Although some tarot cartomancy occurred in Bologna, it was French fortune-tellers like Jean-Baptiste Alliette who first wrote about the version of tarot reading that we are familiar with today, including some of the key spreads we are familiar with and the names Minor Arcana and Major Arcana for different sets of cards. These fortune-tellers started out ascribing meanings to the cards in the common Piquet playing card pack, then shuffling these cards, spreading them out in prescribed formats, and telling the future based on which cards were revealed. Jean-Baptiste— known by his alias Etteilla while fortune-telling— transferred this approach to cartomancy to the tarot deck. By this time, these cards were no longer used commonly in France for trick-taking games, so they seemed mysterious and exotic to the general population, adding to the appeal.

Etteilla popularised the theories of Protestant pastor Antoine Court de Gébelin, who originally claimed tarot could be traced back to ancient Egyptian symbolism.[155] As late as the 1780s, it was still common for European intellectuals to believe that the hieroglyphics of ancient Egyptians held insights into human existence.[155] The meaning of Egyptian writing was unable to be translated until the Rosetta Stone was rediscovered in 1799, and the mystery of hieroglyphics held a magical appeal. This meant that linking tarot imagery to Egyptian symbolism gave cartomancy with this deck more credibility, and deliberately obfuscated the deck's actual history.[156,146]

This obfuscation of knowledge is another reason why researching practices before incorporating them into your own eclectic pagan faith can be challenging. Unlike spiritually significant items like white sage and palo santo, tarot cards are not considered a closed practice. However, some people with a misunderstanding of tarot's history have claimed otherwise, believing only particular cultural groups are sanctioned to use the cards. One common misconception is tarot reading is a closed practice of the Romani people. Although Romani fortune tellers did adopt the use of tarot cards from the 18th century, the closed practice is not the cards themselves but the specific style of cartomancy they developed—referred to as *Dukkering* or *Bocht*—which they continue to pass down through oral tradition and use today.[157]

Despite deliberate attempts by Western Europeans like Etteilla to make fortune-telling seem mysterious, most tarot readers in the 1700s did not claim their readings were derived from arcane knowledge. Although a few fortune-tellers belonged to secret societies or claimed to have ancient wisdom, many were proud to share that their tarot readings were based on their intuitions and varied greatly from practitioner to practitioner.[146]

It was only as French tarotists began to influence England in the late 1800s that more standardised meanings started to emerge. Some members of the Hermetic Order of the Golden Dawn—a prominent occultist group—designed the first set of English tarot cards and, with them, published a set of card meanings.[146] This led to English speakers treating tarot readings as uniform and devaluing the intuitive aspects of the craft.[146] (The Hermetic Order of the Golden Dawn had prominent occultists Aleister Crowley and Lady Frieda Harris among its members, who also published another lesser known but still popular cartomancy deck called the Thoth deck.)[146]

The tarot deck popularised by the Hermetic Order of the Golden Dawn featured images most of us associate with tarot now. This deck—originally known as the Rider-Waite deck—was first published in 1909 and is named after William Rider (the publisher) and Arthur Edward Waite (who was inspired to create the deck after visiting a photography exhibition of the oldest completely illustrated French tarot deck, the Sola-Busca).[158] Waite wrote the accompanying book of card meanings that was published with the English translation. The original name of the Rider-Waite deck completely erases Pamela Colman

Smith, whose art is the reason the deck was so successful and remains the cornerstone of tarot discourse today.[159] Smith was an incredible artist who was known to mobilise women's art to serve as propaganda for the suffrage movement.[160,183] Thankfully, some modern publishings of this deck correct this error by changing its name to the Rider-Waite-Smith, or simply Waite-Smith, deck.[159]

Despite being published in 1909, tarot didn't become globally popular until the Rider-Waite-Smith deck was republished by Stuart R Kaplan in the United States in 1971.[161] The New Age movement in the 1970s was the perfect environment to cultivate interest in fortune-telling, and the popularity of the Rider-Waite-Smith deck was followed by an onslaught of different tarot and oracle decks with different authors, artists, expansions, and subtle differences, based on the interpretations of each deck's creators.[162]

As the French tarotists understood: interpretation is key. Tarot may or may not offer true fortune-telling powers, but it can act as a powerful reflective tool. The cards can be used as a focal point during therapy, counselling, or chaplaincy, offering an individual guidance in forming connections between otherwise disparate and disorderly thoughts and emotions.[163] Tarot is being leveraged in collaborative psychology and psychotherapy, as a way to support clients in verbalising and exploring subjects that they are otherwise unable or unwilling to articulate.[164] The cards can help a querent consciously understand or accept an idea that they already know subconsciously, and thus "motivate emotional, cognitive, or behavioural change".[163]

Use of tarot decks has also been recommended to clients as a creative way to practise self-reflection, meditation, and mindfulness when acting as both the querent and reader.[165] In a quantitative study about this experimental practice, 80% of the clients surveyed felt that using tarot in their sessions contributed to achieving their individual purpose and goals, and 93% felt their reading was "meaningful and significant".[163]

This parallels my experience with using tarot cards.

As part of my travels to the United Kingdom in 2019, I visited Sussex, England on a spiritual pilgrimage. I spent four days staying at a bed-and-breakfast on a hillside with a small group of incredible women and nonbinary folk. While I was there, I read tarot for my fellow pilgrims and taught them how to interpret the cards. I felt privileged to contribute to what was already a reflective and healing experience for all of us. One of the coordinators of the pilgrimage—a secular chaplain named Vanessa—referred to the work I was doing as a type of chaplaincy.

Australia has an interesting relationship with chaplaincy. Since October 2006, Australia has had some form of national chaplaincy program for state schools. The program allows schools to hire chaplains to "support the wellbeing of students and school communities through pastoral care services and student support strategies".[166] Although chaplains, in this context, are essentially asked to perform activities associated with secular youth workers, many of the organisations tasked with hiring chaplains and placing them in public schools have Christian affiliations.[167] (Although some try to disguise this affiliation, like the National School Chaplaincy Association who share detailed census data and FAQs about chaplaincy but keep disclaimers like "The National School Chaplaincy Association [NSCA] is a network of Christian Chaplaincy organisations in Australia"[168] in very small writing at the bottom of their infographics).

When I taught high school students in the early 2010s, I encountered chaplains at two of the schools I worked at. Both of these chaplains were Christian, and were forthright about their faith—with myself and with my students. There were strong parallels between the way these chaplains practised and the spiritual guidance that the Associate Principal of Religious Education would offer students at the Catholic schools I attended. This aligns with reports others have shared about school chaplains in Australian schools, with "chaplains being encouraged to promote a Christian theology course to students in NSW",[169] and instances where chaplains struggle to support students with particular identities and situations if they do not align with their beliefs. There are similar concerns in other areas that employ chaplains, like the Australian Defense Force, where members may have trouble discussing "abortion, contraception, sex outside marriage and marriage breakdown"[170] due to bias, or perceived bias, based on the chaplain's beliefs.

My experiences with chaplaincy in Australia were the reason I was surprised when I met Vanessa in Sussex; she was the first secular chaplain I'd ever encountered. She is an atheist, but culturally

Jewish, and approaches every conversation with an open heart. She focuses on the needs and beliefs of the person speaking to her rather than her own, like a counsellor or social worker who has extra expertise on big spiritual questions like purpose, connection, and ritual. Working with Vanessa led me to research chaplaincy and I discovered that, contrary to my assumptions, all chaplains should be "dedicated to interfaith ministry".[171] Just as a good psychologist asks questions, presents frameworks and knowledge, and allows a client to find their own solutions rather than dictating next steps, a good chaplain acts as a mirror to a person's own spiritual beliefs and asks them insightful questions that help them to reach answers on their own. Learning this ultimately led to me pursuing studies to become a qualified chaplain myself, honing the spiritual counselling skills that I was previously intuiting. Although I don't work as a chaplain, the skills I developed during the course have been invaluable in both my professional and personal life for understanding how to reflect a person's own situation back to them and help them navigate challenges without imposing my own beliefs, ideas, and suggestions upon them. One of the tools I use to help with this process is tarot.

I am not the only person who uses tarot as a chaplaincy tool. In 2017, the University of Alberta was one of three universities in Canada who had a Wiccan chaplain, and he used tarot readings to engage with students of all faiths.[172,173] Pagan chaplains are still uncommon, but they are starting to be hired in spaces where chaplains are employed, including universities, prisons, and hospitals.[174-176]

There is also an international organisation dedicated to the support of pagan chaplains.[177]

And this support is needed, as changes to our societal understanding of who can be a chaplain and how they can serve their community are slow and not without challenges. Pagan chaplains are often assumed to be Christian due to a lack of understanding about what modern chaplaincy involves, can have their faith challenged by the people they are trying to help, and are actively banned from working in certain spaces like the United States military.[176,172] (The US military has adapted somewhat since dismissing a chaplain for converting to Wiccan in 2006, and has allowed the Wiccan pentacle symbol on graves since 2007, and permitted military personnel to list their faith as pagan, Wiccan, Druid, or Heathen in official documents since 2017).[178-181]

Expanding my understanding of chaplaincy as a way to show compassion, rather than a way to proselytise religious beliefs, has impacted how I move through the world. Since working with, and learning from, Vanessa in Sussex, she has invited me to speak to classes she runs about the benefits and techniques of using tarot for self-reflection. This has allowed me to approach tarot with more intentionality and consciousness about how to use it as a spiritual tool, as well as how to provoke curiosity in others who might see a purpose for it within their own spiritual practice.

Although this explicit understanding of tarot as chaplaincy is new, my use of cards is not. I've been reading tarot, and other oracle cards, for people for over a decade. Or perhaps it is more accurate to say I read tarot *with* others. It's vital when reading tarot, or performing any type of chaplaincy, to work together to create interpretations that make sense and provide significance, rather than simply telling the querent what to do.[163] As such, there is no right or wrong way to read tarot. Those who insist there is a correct way to interpret the cards are generally referring to the text written by Arthur Edward Waite in the early 1900s (which disregards the interpretative practices of the French that came before it), or to the work of Jean-Baptiste Alliette in the late 1700s (who lied about the cartomancy origins of tarot), both of whom I feel comfortable ignoring. For the most part, if a tarot or oracle deck is accompanied by a book that declares how you *must* interpret its cards, I promptly put it down again.

Still, I enjoy reading different tarot guidebooks and seeing the ways that others interpret these cards. They may not have been used for cartomancy for thousands of years, but these images and illustrations have been reimagined in thousands of ways, and I find those variations of human expression fascinating.

For some people, reading tarot must be a time-consuming and ritualised practice, whereas for others it can be a half-distracted act as you head out the door to work in the morning. Some insist that you should ask the cards a question before a reading, use a specific spread or pattern of drawing the cards, and give different meanings or significance to upright and reversed cards (i.e. cards that are drawn upside down). Many guidebooks define the meanings of different cards individually, but don't talk about how to interpret the cards as a holistic picture—which I feel is like describing the taste of each individual ingredient and then expecting a person to understand the overall flavour of the meal they comprise. Some decks reinvent their illustrations to introduce more women than the original Rider-Waite-Smith deck or to add people of colour, while other decks change the illustrations of people into something else entirely, like flowers, cats, or characters from *Buffy the Vampire Slayer*.[182-185]

The endless iterations of how to use tarot—and how to practise paganism generally—is what makes me love this approach to faith. There are so many ways to adapt pagan beliefs to your own context and life, from renaming the moons to changing the traditions of sabbat celebrations. There are many ways to research and interpret history, and apply your findings to your way of seeing the world.

However, the growing popularity of paganism and similar faiths has led to a disconnection between what we do and why we do it. With Gerald Gardner inventing a fake history for Wicca to absolve himself of responsibility, occultists manipulating the history of tarot to make it seem more exotic, white supremacists deliberately appropriating Norse history for their political ends, and the modern wellness industry using white sage and palo santo without understanding its cultural significance or environmental impacts, it's easy for the satisfaction of reconnecting with the Earth to get lost in the noise. This applies to all facets of paganism, but it also applies more widely: we have so many sources of information to sort through daily as we try to make decisions about our faith, our health, and even our housework.

BODIES, HOMES, AND GENDER ROLES

I have always had an inconsistent relationship with tasks like cooking and cleaning. I like having a tidy home, but I'm uninspired by the laundry. Some days baking new things excites me, but I'm always plagued by the question, "What should we have for dinner?" Despite knowing objectively that the gendered division of household labour is ridiculous, I still feel especially guilty when I don't have time to sweep the floors or load the dishwasher because it's my *responsibility* as a woman to keep the house clean—even though I also work a full time job.

Homemaking is tangled up in ideas of morality, pride, guilt, and shame. It is a common experience for people, especially women, to feel like their worth is directly tied to the cleanliness of their house.[186] If we don't manage to keep our home at a standard we believe is high enough, we can feel so much shame that it paralyses us and makes it impossible to tidy up, creating a cyclical problem. This makes us tend to our homes—not because we want to feel ownership and joy regarding our space, but because we feel obligated for our home to look a particular way for the sake of a broader society, who often isn't even invited through the front door.

The relationship between our private sphere and our virtues is one that the wellness industry weaponises. There's a pervasive idea that spending an excessive amount of time thinking about how to eat, drink, move around, think, and *breathe* is somehow a virtuous act.[187] It's empowering to realise we can take charge of our lives and the choices we make every day. However, the self-help mindset can distract us from wider societal issues and lead to feelings of guilt and blame about who we are as individuals. When we are asked to find individual solutions to collective problems, we can begin to feel as though we are personally at fault for inequalities that we could—and should—be solving together.[13]

The self-help and wellness industries work as follows: they convince us there is a problem, something is wrong with us, or something is missing. Next, they amplify the guilt and shame that we are perfectly capable of developing on our own if we leave dirty dishes in the sink overnight or haven't been to the gym in a week. Finally, we are shown a simple solution in the form of a product, service, or subscription that we need to spend money on. But the solution doesn't work— and that's by design. If we actually solve our problems, then the wellness industry is no longer able to leverage those problems to sell us things, and the entire system falls apart.[29]

Although the self-help, wellness, and diet industries are not synonymous, there's a lot of crossover in their Venn diagrams. (This is not a completely accurate use of the term Venn diagram, but you understand what I mean).[188] The diet industry follows a similar model, using our guilt and shame to make us pay for ways to become thinner, under the guise of actually becoming healthier or morally better. We are forced to make choices about what we eat every day while we are bombarded with food pyramids, calorie counts on takeaway meals, and recommended daily allowances of macronutrients on the back of food packets.

But nutritional science is still a relatively new field of study—the first vitamin was only chemically isolated in 1926—and has been influenced by political factors, capitalist motivations, and both conscious and unconscious biases.[189] As science develops and political agendas change, the morality of our food choices changes with it. We see it in our news media all the time, with reports on each new scientific study simplifying preliminary population-level observations into individual mandates: we *should* eat fish, we *shouldn't* eat fish; we *should* drink coffee, we *shouldn't* drink coffee, and so on.[190] Studies have found that this contradictory information means people feel confused about how to maintain and improve their health, even beyond the topics they're reading about.190 It can make it hard to trust even the most certain information, like the advice that vegetables and exercise are good for us.[190]

We assume the measures we use to assess our food choices—some of which we've been taught since we were children and that have been the basis of widespread public policy—are scientifically proven, accurate, or at least *useful*. However, examples like the food pyramid, calories, and daily allowances all become more complicated when scrutinised. A meta-analysis of 39 studies across 59 restaurant chains shows that calorie labelling on menus has no effect on calorie consumption (and the relationship between calorie consumption, weight, and health is more complicated than most people seem to recognise, anyway).[191,192] The widely known food pyramid isn't representative of the original research conducted into portion sizing, and was heavily influenced by the interests of lobby groups and produce farmers including dairy, meat, and wheat growers.[193] Recommended allowances for food have only been around since World War II, and were originally created because there was an increased interest in the *minimum* amount of food a person could survive on when there was an influx of refugees in places like North America.[187] They were not created as a measure for a reasonable and healthy amount the average person should eat in a day and should never have been widely adopted for that purpose.[187] Our medical practitioners often don't have a comprehensive understanding of these misconceptions,[194] so what hope does the average person have?

The key takeaway here is that we shouldn't tie our worth as people to the food choices we make—especially when the research we are using to inform our decisions is complicated, messy, poorly communicated by the press, and designed to teach us about the overall human population, not the choices we make for our own lives.[187] And yet, despite knowing this and confidently suggesting you apply this lens to your own life, I still find myself slipping back into that pattern no matter how hard I try to disentangle myself from it—the same way I find myself feeling guilty about when I last did a load of laundry.

As I started contemplating the framework of guilt and shame we build around food, I realised I have a complicated, and previously unspoken, internal ranking system for different meals. Home-cooked meals that are made from scratch and are full of vegetables are the best, of course—especially if they have more green vegetables and fewer starchy ones. This is followed by pre-made but home-prepared meals, like microwavable frozen meals. Eating out at a restaurant or at the park is better than getting takeaway and eating it at home, even though the nutritional value and the price of the food is the exact same. Takeaway is still morally better if I go to the location and pick it up myself, rather than getting it delivered.

You might read this and think it's ridiculous that I've mapped it out so thoroughly. You might be nodding along thinking, "yes, that is the correct ranking", or you may disagree with my assessment of which meals should make us feel guiltiest. Regardless of your response, I guarantee you have assigned moral value to some foods or ways of eating, and I encourage you to spend a moment interrogating those feelings, where they came from, and if they're true.

Even now that I've reflected on these arbitrary rules I have assigned to food choices in my life, I still don't fully understand how they have become so embedded in my brain. Mostly, I think

they have been there since my first foray into
autonomous adulthood, which I assume is due
to some combination of my family's values and
society's expectations. I remember the first time
I went on vacation with my now-husband, we
decided to order pizza to the hotel room where we
were staying. I thought we were being incredibly
naughty because prior to that night in my early 20s,
I had never ordered delivery before. In this modern
world of delivery apps, that almost seems as foreign
as remembering when we couldn't use the internet
to stream music or access our bank balance. But
why do I associate a moral value with one and not
the others?

Studies show I'm not the only person whose
meals are governed by unspoken rules and
influenced by guilt, although the specifics vary.
People care about how they eat and provide for
their families, and across all income levels they
"feel like they're failing"[195] because they are trying
to meet an impossible standard. We are inundated
by books, articles, and television shows about how
home-cooked meals are not only morally better
than takeaway, but they're also *easy*. Websites are
full of recipes that supposedly take only thirty
minutes to prepare and use four ingredients or
less. Or maybe you can just prep all your meals
on the weekend so they're ready to go during the
week. What about subscribing to a meal box service
that will send you all the ingredients, perfectly
proportioned? And just look at all of our kitchen
gadgets!

And by gadgets, I don't just mean things like
egg cubers,[196] which turn hard-boiled eggs into

cubes after cooking so that they can be... square, I guess? In addition to egg cubers, we generally have electricity, plumbing, and appliances in Western society that, theoretically, make it simpler to prepare a home-cooked meal than it was in our great-grandmothers' times. Between the late 1800s and early 1900s (the second industrial revolution), society's obsession with standardisation and efficiency led to a boom in household appliances.[197] For example, the vacuum cleaner became available in 1913, the washing machine in 1916, and the refrigerator in 1918.[198] However, these appliances were still inaccessibly expensive for a lot of households, or required running water and electricity to run, which not every household had yet.

Before 1900, many households still relied on manual methods of accessing energy and water, like gas, kerosene, coal, firewood, rainwater tanks, and wells.[199,200] Appliances were made more convenient following World War II, with post-war innovations in technology making existing machines more affordable and inspiring new technologies.[198] As power stations were built, electricity became cheaper and more reliable, and state governments campaigned for more people to wire up their homes, especially in cities where infrastructure density meant it was possible to connect more households with fewer resources.[199] By the end of the 1950s, electric fridges, washing machines, and stoves had become standard household items. Houses built in Australia started to be equipped with kitchens inspired by the Frankfurt kitchen, which was originally designed in 1926 but was unable to be widely implemented until white goods became a common component of the household kitchen.[201] The Frankfurt kitchen began revolutionising kitchens in North America around the same time.

The Frankfurt kitchen was designed to create a space that took full advantage of modern household appliances. Following World War I, social housing projects became common in German cities as a way to address the housing shortage for the working class. These projects tended to contain large numbers of small, affordable apartments that followed near-identical floor plans, and architects had to figure out ways to create comfortable, efficient spaces for those families to use. Margarete Schütte-Lihotzky—considered to be "the first professional female architect in Austria"[202]— designed what is now known as the Frankfurt kitchen for a social housing project created by Ernst May in Frankfurt, Germany.

Schütte-Lihotzky's kitchen prioritised cleanliness and productivity. The cabinets were made of softwood and plywood, with beech and linoleum work surfaces to maintain hygiene and protect against stains and knife marks.[202,203] The compact design also included a revolving stool, removable garbage drawer, and drawers for storing kitchen staples like flour and sugar. Although the kitchens in the final housing project were a variety of colours, the first prototype was "painted monochrome blue due to the fact that flies don't perceive it as solid and are therefore discouraged from landing on the surface".[203] Schütte-Lihotzky had never run a household before designing the

Frankfurt kitchen, so she interviewed housewives and women's groups about their priorities, used a stopwatch to assess how long women spent on each food preparation task, and was inspired by railway dining cars where two cooks could efficiently prepare meals for nearly 100 passengers.[202,203]

The Frankfurt kitchen was revolutionary—and not just because it included a gas stove. At this point in history, it was practically unheard of for women to be directly consulted on issues that would impact their lives.[202] There is a similar problem with the moral arguments for home-cooking today: the public figures who prescribe correct cooking and eating behaviours are mostly white, mostly male, and their ideals rarely work when applied to the real life experiences of marginalised people and the intersectional population.[195]

There is a pervasive idea that women should not work or that they belong in the kitchen, with research showing that these misogynistic ideas are as common now as they were thirty years ago.[204] However, this myth requires us to subscribe to a heteronormative understanding of gender and relationships. Although I am a woman in a relationship with a man, my bisexuality and my active involvement in the queer community has helped me question my assumptions about what it means to identify with a particular gender, to be in a relationship, and to choose your role on a team based on mutual respect between partners rather than a gender-based set of expectations assigned at birth.

However, even without the queer destabilisation

of gender, sexuality, and monogamy, the assumption that heterosexual couples have which, until very recently, featured a woman who tended to the home while their husband went to work is still simply *false*. Before World War I, kitchens were spaces only occupied by the lower classes. Families unable to afford servants cooked for themselves in unhygienic spaces that lacked room for preparation or any modern appliances.[202] Generally, the women in these households would work—sometimes as domestic servants themselves—to afford food and shelter. For wealthy families, kitchens were hidden in the basement and were used by servants, who prepared meals before bringing them upstairs.[202] Between 1880 and 1940, almost all upper- and middle-class families in America employed at least one domestic servant, with domestic service being the most common job among wage-earning women.[195,205] In Australia, domestic service was even more common than in the United States, until 1940 when the industry began to decline.[206]

The adoption of Schütte-Lihotzky's design in kitchens across the Western world caused an unprecedented class shift in the expectations of women as home cooks. The kitchen was raised out of the basement and cooking was suddenly treated as commendable—and visible—labour.[202] Middle-class and wealthy women started spending more time in their kitchens, and trade shows full of modern appliances were exciting places to visit. In Melbourne, people would visit All Electrical fairs to look at demonstrations of fancy new household inventions.[207] The time a wife spent in the kitchen started to become a marker of their wealth rather than poverty because, in post-war Western society, it was an indicator of financial security if a family did not need the woman of the house to be earning a second income.[202] By 1979, the number of wage-earning women employed as domestic workers had reduced from 50% to 3%.[205] By 2001, only one in approximately 162 households employed a domestic servant.[195]

Sometimes we incorrectly imagine that every Western woman in the mid-1900s was a white-apron-wearing housewife who spent every idyllic day baking bread, tidying the house, and caring for their children like characters in *The Stepford Wives*.[208] However, many women in Western countries started working during the World Wars to support military efforts and continued engaging in paid employment during peacetime to further assist their families, as well as gain some independence.[209] Although careers in more "prestigious professions" (law, academia, business)[209] were still largely reserved for men,—who remained the breadwinners—women were allowed to work "little jobs".[209] In 1900, only 5% of married women in the United States were working for a wage, and this had increased to 61% by 2000.[210] In Britain, 20% of women were working for a wage in 1951 and this rose to almost 50% in 1971.[209]

Basically, since the beginning of the contemporary kitchen, and even before that, many women have been juggling the responsibilities of paid work and housework. And, for just as long, women have been feeling guilty about not doing enough, doing too much, or doing the wrong things. The common narrative that we are failing

our families and need to return to the ways of
our great-grandmothers is a myth; overall, we
are healthier and living longer today than three
generations ago, and our diets are a significant
contributor to that. The narrative that women used
to home cook all their meals is a myth too; many
Americans used to rely on low-income people of
colour to prepare their food. And they still do.
The only difference is that, instead of working as
domestic servants, these people of colour now work
in restaurants and as food delivery drivers.[195]

There is a moral issue with buying food
from restaurants or ordering delivery, but it's
not the issue that the media tends to suggest.
Books, articles, and motivational talks claim
that individuals should be able to make time to
cook food, and make us feel guilty if we fail. In a
presentation in Vancouver, Michael Pollan—a
speaker and author whose work focuses on food—
responded to an audience question by saying,
"We're going to have to fix our diet before we fix the
whole economy."[195] But this is exactly the opposite
approach we should be taking. We are asking
individuals to take on the responsibility of caring
for their families in a system that doesn't facilitate
that, and then making them feel guilty when they
inevitably fail. The moral issue with eating at
restaurants or getting our meals delivered isn't
that we have failed to cook dinner and therefore
our families will be unhealthy, our budgets will
be damaged, and our great-grandmothers would
be ashamed of us. The issue is that the hospitality
industry exploits its workers and we are operating
within that immoral system.[195] But cooking our

own food won't solve that problem either; the low-income workers in the grocery stores where we often source our ingredients are working in similarly poor conditions.[195]

Some individual decisions may help improve the situation. For example, favouring small businesses and local farmers markets may be a better moral choice, as it financially supports people who are less likely to exploit their workers. We have also been taught shopping locally is a better environmental choice: a majority of people believe buying from local businesses and "reducing food miles" is better for the climate than purchasing food from larger chains, but this isn't necessarily true.[211] What we choose to buy is significantly more important to our overall carbon footprint than where that food is sourced from, with food transportation contributing a tiny percentage to the environmental impact of our food when compared to the farming practices used to grow it.[211] Shopping locally can also be far more expensive than visiting a local chain, which makes it inaccessible to many families, so heralding it as morally superior creates yet another source of guilt that disproportionately targets marginalised people.

Ultimately, it should not be the responsibility of individuals to fix systemic, societal problems. For solutions to be effective, we need policy-makers to create legislation requiring major companies to change the way they operate.[212] Still, it can be empowering to feel like we have agency in making *better* decisions for ourselves and our families. If we are in the financial position to do so, then going to the local farmers market might help us feel like we have a sense of control over our choices and our food, are supporting our community, and choosing to be healthy. If we have the time, then meal prepping on the weekend might help us feel like we have a handle on our lives.[195]

I live close to a market and I love walking there occasionally to buy fresh pasta; the issues arise when I start to feel guilty on weekends when I don't have the time or energy to make the trek. It is important to unpack why our behaviour makes us feel good. Rather than acting to avoid feeling judged by others, to make ourselves feel superior, or to circumvent a misplaced sense of inadequacy in ourselves, we need to be motivated by constructive reasons, such as our sense of routine, feelings of security, or the fact that fresh pasta is *really yummy*.

If we are trying to create new habits in our lives for the wrong reasons, while we can feel empowered for a time, when these routines struggle to stand up to the systems we exist within, we suddenly feel shame and guilt again. For example, during 2021 I started baking bread every weekend (along with a significant percentage of the population who were bored during ongoing pandemic lockdowns).[213] I had always loved baking, but when I moved into my new apartment—complete with a lovely wide counter, perfect for kneading dough—I realised I finally had the space to bake regularly without needing to lock myself in a cramped kitchen space that I didn't enjoy. I was proud of myself for being consistent with baking every weekend for about a year, but then my priorities shifted and I started buying sourdough from the bakery on weekends instead. The sourdough is delicious, but immediately a sense of guilt crept in and I had to negotiate with myself to ignore it. Our sense of control over our individual food routines and decisions is precarious.[195]

Even though I don't bake bread every weekend right now, I still love baking. Kneading dough helps me feel connected to the Earth, gives me an opportunity to be mindful and reflective, and reminds me that I am part of a long lineage of people who have been making bread by hand for generations. But I also realise I make bread a little differently to how we were able to only a few generations ago: I fill a cup with warm water from the tap and put dehydrated yeast in to let it activate, then I add store-bought flour and semolina and set my standing mixer to run. Once the dough has come together, I knead it by hand before putting it aside to rest. I use my smartwatch to set timers so I remember to check on the dough after each proving stage. Once the dough is ready, I put the loaves in the electric oven and wash the bowl in the dishwasher. Making bread isn't easy or quick—it still takes some elbow grease, and I have to commit to staying home for at least two hours to see the loaves through from beginning to end. But these modern technologies make the process far easier than it would have been for my great-grandmother.

Prior to industrialisation, baking bread was a family affair for those who were unable to afford a domestic servant. Most households grew their own crops that could be harvested for grain like corn, and this was collected, shelled, and pounded into cornmeal by the husband before the wife turned that cornmeal into bread.[214] Cornbread was originally a common staple in African-American households; recipes spread from there to the families they laboured for, and then were passed between white households until cornbread became a tradition across the American South.[215]

Grain-related chores were difficult and time-consuming. Some families had handmills they could operate at home while others had to take a cart to a nearby watermill; either way, the husband had to conduct this process at regular intervals to ensure the family had enough flour to cook their meals.[214] Although corn, as well as rye and wheat, would keep indefinitely once they had been harvested and dried, they were more perishable as meals and flours so only small quantities could be milled at a time.[214] Fine white flour would last longer than other meals but it couldn't be made using a handmill, and the same quantity of grain would produce less white flour at the watermill than other crops, so it was an inefficient choice when carting quantities of grain back and forth.[214]

Merchants in America began milling flour to sell in the late 1700s, but this was mostly a product for exporting to Europe at first. Flour and meal were "the second most important American export product[s]"[214] at the time, following tobacco. The Europeans relied on flour, and the British made wheat production a staple industry in Australia from the moment they first arrived in 1788, bringing wheat seeds and stone mills with them.[216] Over time, flour became more prevalent and a surplus of merchant-milled white flour developed in America. Coupled with better transportation options, it became possible to carry pre-milled flour over distances cheaply and quickly. Suddenly, store-bought flours were available and affordable for families, and one of the most time-consuming household chores disappeared.[214]

However, this burden was not reduced equally: men no longer needed to spend days at a time tending to, harvesting, and milling grains, but women were still expected to bake bread from the store-bought flours. In fact, women were now expected to do more labour than before. When relying on home-grown grains, corn was the most common grain ingredient used for making bread in America.[214] Cornmeal is easy to bake with: you add a liquid and leavening, then you bake or fry the dough. Doughs made from cornmeal don't need yeast, don't need to prove, and kneading is not recommended. But once wheat flour could be purchased, white bread became a symbol of wealth because it signified that people had the money required to buy the fine white flour, and also that a man's wife (or servants) had the spare time required to prepare it.[214] Cornbread became stigmatised due to its associations with specific cultures and classes, and this stigmatisation remains today.[217]

Cornbread is not the only delicious foodstuff that has been stigmatised due to its cultural and socioeconomic ties. One of my favourite vegetables is the potato, but ongoing elitism regarding this delicious and versatile root has led to me feeling guilty whenever I incorporate it in my meals (which is often). In the mid-1800s, science began to understand that the nutrients people consumed impacted their ability to function in a variety of ways.[221] Although the specifics were still a mystery, people started to associate the behaviours of certain groups to the foods they were eating. Potatoes were a staple of the working class diet in the United Kingdom, with one in three people relying on potatoes year-round in Ireland.[218] This reliance was the reason that, when a disease known as the Blight began affecting Irish potatoes in the mid-1800s, it ultimately led to the death of more than one million Irish people, with two million more fleeing the country in search of sustenance.[219]

Although the Blight was the initial cause of what is now known as the Great Famine or the Potato Famine, it was exacerbated by the Whig administration in London refusing to intervene with economic support and continuing to allow the export of grain and livestock from Ireland.[220] The primary justification for the Whig Party's indifference to the significant plight of the Irish was the belief that the Irish were inferior to the English, and lacked moral character.[220] The association between potatoes and the working class, coupled with the industrialised system condemning the "laziness"[221] of Irish workers, meant the potato was blamed for not providing people with adequate nutrition.

However, potatoes are actually nutritionally rich—which we learned once we isolated vitamins and minerals in the early 1900s.[189] Potatoes are a source of potassium, dietary fibre, iron, vitamin C, B vitamins, calcium, magnesium, phosphorus, and more.[222-224] In fact, a single serving of some potato varieties can constitute approximately 8% of an adult's daily iron intake, 12% of their dietary fibre, and 19% of their potassium. Potatoes have been associated with obesity and diabetes, but there's a lack of scientific data supporting these claims.[222] Part of the reason potatoes are associated with these outcomes is because they contain carbohydrates (as does lettuce, green beans, and kale), and many contemporary fad diets claim carbohydrates cause weight gain.[223] However, there is no scientific evidence that a low-carb diet consistently improves weight management, leads to weight loss, or makes a person healthier.[225]

Meanwhile, potatoes have been shown to have a positive impact on blood pressure and satiety (i.e. the sensation of feeling full and satisfied).[222] Their naturally high fibre content can help with lowering a person's risk of heart disease, stroke, type 2 diabetes, and bowel cancer.[224] Potatoes are also naturally gluten-free, which helps people with coeliac disease, and are a recommended option for people with gut issues like irritable bowel syndrome (IBS).[224] IBS is a symptom of my fibromyalgia, and potatoes are one of the most reliable meals I can eat while I'm having a flare-up. Tossing some frozen chips into the air-fryer is quick and easy if I'm in pain, doesn't require me to add any additional fat to this naturally fat-free vegetable, and rarely aggravates my IBS further. As somebody who was also a selective eater as a child—and still has trouble with the taste and texture of many foods today—I often relied on a side of hot chips with meals so I had a palate cleanser between bites. This isn't an uncommon preference for picky eaters—fries have an excellent crunchy and soft texture, a relatively plain but salty flavour, and a pleasantly neutral colour. There's a reason they're still my safe food.

The fact that potatoes have been depicted as an unhealthy and lower-class choice in Western society discourages people from relying on a vegetable that is affordable, easy to cook, and has several health benefits. When we finally let ourselves order a meal with a side of chips instead of a salad, we feel ashamed. Shame has been impacting what we cook and how we eat for years. When the time women spent in the kitchen became an indicator of a family's class in the 1900s, convenient, easy-to-cook options became unpopular. Instead, the media marketed foods that required women to spend more time and physical exertion in the kitchen, and these trends continue to influence our sense of self-worth today.

Innovations in appliances have saved women some time around the house. In 1900, a woman spent 58 hours per week on household chores, compared to 18 hours per week in 1975.[198,210] Another study found that in 1924, 87% of married women in Middletown, Indiana were spending more than four hours per day doing housework. By 1999, only 14% of women said they spent more than four hours on housework per day and 33% said they did less than an hour per day.[210] This makes some sense: it's quicker to buy kerosene for lamps than make your own candles or to purchase pre-made cotton for sewing rather than needing to comb, card, spin, and weave it yourself.[214] It's even quicker to have electrical lights and store-bought clothing.

However, technological progress hasn't freed women in the way they were promised.[226] With each improvement in household technology, there is a corresponding increase in expectations for women—an impact not shared by men. Many of the time-saving appliances installed in homes simply reorganised the work women were expected to complete, rather than reducing their labour.[214] For example, in 1884 the egg beater was patented.[227] Before its invention, it could take up to 45 minutes to work eggs and butter together with a spoon or by hand until they were aerated, so the beater was surely guaranteed to save a housewife time. However, the first recipe of the angel food cake was also published in 1884 and became instantly popular.[228] Angel food cakes require egg whites to be separated from egg yolks and beaten separately, doubling the work. This is a perfect example of a woman gaining access to a labour-saving device and immediately experiencing societal pressure that seeks to domesticate and subdue her, making her do more labour. It's such a quintessential example that the podcast that introduced me to the story originally suggested that this set of circumstances should be called "the egg-beater effect".[226]

Society has taught us that doing things the hard way is somehow morally better than "taking the easy way out", despite the fact we now have access to technology that gives us easy ways to do tasks that our great-grandmothers were doing by hand. But hand-washing dishes isn't somehow morally better than using a dishwasher, and dishwashers use less water anyway.[229]

Still, if hand-washing dishes is a meditative activity for you, or it's the best time for you to listen to your favourite podcast, don't let the environmental benefits of dishwashers guilt you into changing your routine. There are pagans and witches who use the time they spend with their hands in water as an opportunity for everyday ritual: pausing, breathing, connecting to the Earth, and cleansing themselves along with their plates and cutlery, and feeling connected to nature in this way has other benefits too.[230] Remember that societal problems are best solved at the societal level; as an individual, you can address climate change more effectively by writing to your local politicians than by saving a little water each time you do a load of dishes.

Household tasks like washing dishes are not as inherent to my own spirituality as they might be for a kitchen witch, but there can be something satisfying about doing things with our hands, making something from scratch, and taking time to pause in whatever way most resonates with you. For me, this looks like baking, gardening, and creating art. Using my hands to make beautiful things from nothing—from loaves of bread to crochet baby blankets, from multimedia journal pages to a new leaf unfurling.

I am still learning how to prioritise the acts I find genuinely fulfilling over the tasks I feel obligated to complete, to forgive myself for not enjoying vacuuming, and to remind myself that I am not unvirtuous simply because the house is untidy when guests come to visit. I'm ordering takeaway on nights where I don't have the energy to cook, I'm buying the fancy salted butter instead of the low fat margarine, and I'm using the dishwasher.

Deprogramming decades of societal pressure and

replacing those messages with ones of compassion is challenging, but it's also a radical act of self-love. I deserve to spend less time cleaning the floor and more time looking up at the stars—and so do you.

HYSTERIA, ILLNESS, AND BURNING US ALIVE

I've mentioned a few times now that I have fibromyalgia (or fibro). It's a chronic pain condition that causes widespread aching and soreness through my muscles and joints, as well as all sorts of other symptoms related to my nervous system like gastrointestinal issues, fatigue and other sleep issues, and pins and needles. I liken it to having an enthusiastic goblin who lives inside me and sometimes likes to set things on fire for no discernable reason.

The causes—both of fibromyalgia in general and the intermittent flare-ups that a person with fibro gets—are unknown. The most recent school of thought is that the original onset of fibro is caused by a combination of genetic predisposition and some sort of trauma, stress, or infection.[231] Individuals claim their flare-ups can be attributed to diet, stress, the weather, or pure chance. After years of tracking my symptoms and trying to understand my triggers, I've decided I'm in the *pure chance* category. Although being rundown after periods of high intensity can sometimes increase my chances of experiencing symptoms, it's inconsistent and impossible to predict.

I've been experiencing these symptoms for over a decade, but I was only diagnosed in 2020. Prior to that, I thought my pain and exhaustion was normal, and perhaps I was just less tolerant or resilient than my peers. Everybody experiences sore muscles, fatigue, and the occasional stomach ache, right? So why could they get on with their day while I sometimes struggled to get out of bed?

Maybe I was just being melodramatic or hysterical.

I spent years trying to figure out what was wrong. I went from doctor to doctor, and each one had bright ideas and a little optimism they would be the one to solve the mystery. We discovered some vitamin deficiencies in my early twenties and thought fixing that might do it. Getting vitamin injections helped me with my anxiety, irritability, and fatigue, but didn't solve my pain and digestion issues. One doctor told me about irritable bowel syndrome (IBS) and suggested medications that could help alleviate those symptoms— they were helpful, but not a cure-all. In 2019, a dentist discovered that the right side of my jaw is misaligned. She told me that symptoms like teeth grinding, headaches, nightmares, anxiety, depression, IBS, sinus issues, increased resting heart rate, and pins and needles—all of which I experienced—could be explained by upper airway resistance syndrome (UARS), but a sleep study showed no evidence that this was the cause for me. (I did tongue awareness and Buteyko breathing for a while anyway, just in case it helped.)

When I was 27, ten years after I first started seeking help for my symptoms, I moved to Melbourne and found a new pain specialist. She asked me if I'd ever considered fibromyalgia as the cause of my ongoing issues. I had a couple of friends with fibro, but had never considered I might have the same condition. I went home and read every medical journal article I could find about fibro and discovered the common symptoms, how our understanding of the condition has evolved, and how it's currently impossible to test for. I fell down a research rabbit hole, which took me to the medical journal where the diagnostic criteria for fibromyalgia was published. Within this paper, Table 3 offers readers the complete diagnostic assessment tool that doctors are encouraged to use to check if patients have symptoms associated with fibromyalgia.[232] It was also here I learned that fibromyalgia is entirely invisible to the naked eye and to scans, blood tests, and x-rays. It's a diagnosis by elimination, meaning you need to test for everything else it *could* be before fibro can be considered.[233]

Thankfully, by that point, I had already been tested for a lot. I'd had endoscopies, blood tests, and scans for a decade. I remember once getting a CT scan of my digestive system that required me to drink an expanding orange-flavoured jelly for a couple of hours before the test. It was incredibly unpleasant—both at the time and later that evening. But suddenly this decade of ruling out food allergies, autoimmune conditions, and abnormalities wasn't wasted time. My doctor ran some additional blood tests to check for arthritis markers and asked for an echocardiogram to check for heart conditions, and then worked through the American College of Rheumatology's diagnostic criteria for fibro with me.[232] Ever the high achiever, I aced the test.

As she wrote the word fibromyalgia on my file, my doctor encouraged me to speak to a psychologist after my diagnosis. She told me it would be beneficial to speak about the grief associated with learning my body was chronically ill with a condition that, at least currently, had no cure. But I didn't feel grief; I felt relief. After years of intermittently finding myself in so much pain and despair that I felt caged by my own body, disconnected from nature and isolated from the communities that made me feel like myself, I finally had an explanation. While it didn't magically erase the days where I struggled to fulfil my obligations, engage with my spirituality, or connect with the people around me, it at least helped me feel *seen*. I wasn't being hysterical after all. I had a *real* illness.

Although, the idea of a *real* illness is a little bit hazy. Some doctors still don't consider fibromyalgia to be a real disease, including Dr. Frederick Wolfe, one of the doctors responsible for the diagnostic criteria for fibromyalgia that was first published in 1990.[234] People also thought hysteria was a real malady that afflicted predominantly women from approximately 1900 BCE through to when it was removed from the third edition of the Diagnostic and Statistical Manual of Mental Disorders (DSM-III) in 1980.[235] People all over the world have real symptoms, and are trapped navigating through a world of evolving medical research, incorrect or fake diagnoses, stigma and doubt from others, and an inability to find relief.

The funny thing is many people with fibromyalgia would likely have been diagnosed with hysteria as recently as a hundred years ago. The term fibromyalgia has only existed since 1976, and the first diagnostic criteria for the condition was published in 1990.[284] It's a condition surrounded by debate: is it a pain disease, a brain disease, a small fibre neuropathy, a somatoform pain disorder, a somatic symptom disorder (SSD), or something else entirely?[237]

People are diagnosed with an SSD when they are "excessively distressed"[238] about physical symptoms, which may or may not have any medical explanation, to a point where it disrupts their quality of life. A straight line can be drawn between SSDs and medically diagnosed hysteria. SSDs are an evolution from the somatoform disorders featured in the DSM-IV, with the primary difference being an acknowledgement that the physical symptoms associated with the disorder may have a medical explanation or diagnosis in addition to simply "abnormal thoughts, feelings, and behaviours".[239] The DSM-IV explicitly notes that somatoform disorders were "historically referred to as hysteria". Hysteria evolved into somatoform disorders, which evolved again into somatic symptom disorders. Some experts still believe fibromyalgia can be classified as an SSD.[232] The evolution of hysteria to fibromyalgia in the last hundred years has been swift, and there's a high likelihood that we will learn much more about it during my lifetime.

Similar to fibromyalgia, hysteria had a wide range of symptoms. Some were similar to the fibro symptoms I experience regularly, like muscle pain and spasms, insomnia, and anxiety. Others included irritability, shortness of breath, having too much sex, not having enough sex, infertility, disagreeing with your husband, and a fondness for writing.[241,245] Another common trait between people with hysteria is that they were generally *women*.[241] That's not to say that men weren't just as prone to these behaviours; diagnostic bias around hysteria was caused by "social and political reasons",[242] not an objective assessment of a situation.

Women have often been considered unpredictable and temperamental. The tradition of giving names to tropical cyclones (as well as hurricanes and monsoons) was started by Clement Wragge, a British meteorologist who started naming storms in the late 1800s and early 1900s to make them easier to report on. He chose names based on ancient mythology, specific Polynesian women he was attracted to, and politicians whose policies he disagreed with.[243] But in the 1950s, a more standardised system emerged, which focused exclusively on women's names—a choice that was made supposedly because of women's unpredictable nature.[244] What followed were news reporters speaking about storms as though they were women and exposing their own misogynistic perspectives in the process, calling the storms temperamental or suggesting they were "flirting"[292] with a coastline. The belief that women are hysterical similarly says more about the man diagnosing that woman than it does about the woman herself.

By the 1850s, women could present with one of more than 75 different symptoms and receive a hysteria diagnosis, and by the early 20th century, psychiatrists noted that "any function of the body can be affected by hysteria".[245,247] While some of these patients may have had fibro, it's likely a number of other conditions were being grouped under the hysteria label, including postpartum depression, premenstrual syndrome (PMS), menopause, endometriosis, and other invisible neurological disorders and mental health conditions. For centuries, the label was used as an umbrella to, at best, dismiss the ailments women experienced that medical science didn't understand.[245] At worst, it was used to lock women in asylums to discourage autonomous or rebellious behaviours that were considered wild.[246]

Due to all of the potential symptoms and presentations of hysteria, it was difficult to categorise the condition or determine its cause. Ancient Egyptians and Greeks thought that hysteria was caused by the uterus moving through the body, and used various scents to lure the uterus back into its proper position.[247,249] The term hysteria was coined by Hippocrates in the 5th century BC and literally means "wandering womb".[248] The term derives from *hystericus*, which means of the womb; hysterectomy—the surgical removal of the uterus— is derived from the same Latin root.

Other philosophers and physicians had different theories about the causes and treatments of hysteria, but tended to agree that female sex organs were still to blame. For example, Galen believed the condition was caused by an excess of fluid within the uterus and suggested the only way for this to be cured was for women to have more sex with their husbands to expel what he called—and I'm really sorry for this—the "female seed".[249] Sometimes when I remember this theory and become frustrated, I imagine Galen looking at today's society and becoming overwhelmed by the knowledge that women don't always have uteruses, women sometimes marry other women, women are perfectly capable of orgasming alone, and both hysteria and the gender binary are fake. It makes me feel better.

Fortunately, some people thought these theories about wandering or fluid-filled uteruses were nonsense. Unfortunately, their alternative theories were equally bad. Some people assumed women were more susceptible to hysteria because we are inferior to men, and that this inferiority led to a weakness of both body and spirit. In the 1200s, St. Thomas Aquinas suggested that some women were "evil-minded",[247] a spiritual diagnosis that could be attributed to any woman behaving improperly. The lines between science and demonology blurred at this time; if a woman went to a physician and presented with symptoms that the physician could not attribute to any disease, the Devil was blamed and an exorcism was suggested. The *Malleus Maleficarum*—the primary source on demonology at this time—solidified this recommendation in 1468.[247] (And people wonder why women don't want to go to see a doctor.)

The title *Malleus Maleficarum* is generally translated to Hammer of Witches. Maleficarum is the feminine pluralisation of the word *maleficus*, which refers to a witch, warlock, or sorcerer. The deliberate feminisation of the title immediately positions this book to be about female magic-doers and elevated sorcery to the same level of heresy, which was a criminal offence punishable by death. It suggested that witches should be tortured for information and killed as heretics—which, in the late Middle Ages, involved being burned at the stake.[247]

The *Malleus Maleficarum* spread widely, especially with the invention of the printing press in the 15th century.[250] Between the 15th and 18th centuries, the witch hunts inspired by this book meant thousands of people—mostly women—were killed as a result of confessions obtained through torture.[247] While torture may make it easier to make somebody confess to their supposed crimes, these confessions are often false.[251]

While tracing my own ancestry through the British Isles, I discovered branches of my family tree stretching to Glasgow in the 1600s, where witch trials were common. It's possible that some of my relatives were accused of, or killed for, witchcraft at that time, while others took part in witch hunts against their neighbours. Considering the potential genetic causes of fibromyalgia, perhaps a great-great-great-great-etc grandmother of mine had fibro too, but rather than facing strange medical tests involving orange-flavoured jelly, her inexplicable condition may have been attributed to the Devil instead.

Eventually, physicians decided this theory of hysteria was nonsense (although hysteria, as a condition, was obviously real) and came up with suggestions that shifted the blame from the uterus or demons to the brain and psychology instead. In the 1800s, Jean-Martin Charcot suggested that hysteria was caused by an unknown internal injury that impacted the nervous system.[249] I find this theory particularly interesting, as a misfiring or misinterpretation of the central nervous system is the current most widespread explanation for the constellation of symptoms caused by fibromyalgia as well.[252]

Freud delivered a different theory for hysteria to the medical community in the 1800s: women became hysterical due to the realisation that they had lost their metaphoric phallus.[249] The treatment for this resembled the recommendations made by Galen nearly two thousand years earlier: more heterosexual marriage, followed by heterosexual sex and child-rearing. However, these treatments now supposedly worked for different reasons. Instead of focusing on bodily fluids, Freud believed that these morally righteous practices would help calm women by reuniting them with the phallus they had lost by exposing them to those of their husband and potential sons.[249] Next time somebody refers to "the good old days" or "a simpler time", please remember that less than 200 years ago, researchers could refer to a woman's "metaphoric phallus"[249] at academic conferences with a straight face and people would nod and think "yes, that's a reasonable explanation".

By the late-1800s, an alternative treatment to heterosexual relationships was proposed: hysterical paroxysm. A hysterical paroxysm was achieved through gynaecological massage, either by a doctor or, later, a mechanical device under the supervision of a doctor or a woman's husband.[249,245] Basically, doctors were giving women orgasms to cure hysteria and, in the process, accidentally invented the vibrator. It's theorised that, at the time, men did not consider external stimulation of the clitoris sexual, erotic, or possibly even enjoyable for patients, which says a lot about both the medical system and the patriarchy.[249] Hysterical paroxysms were still a recommended medical treatment as recently as 1910.[249]

Unfortunately, although I have achieved *hysterical paroxysm* many times throughout my life, I still have fibromyalgia. In managing my fibro, I have also tried yoga, meditation, regular exercise, diet changes, cupping, acupuncture, chiropractics, and physiotherapy. I've tried resting through flare-ups, pushing through flare-ups, and screaming at the sky through flare-ups. Some treatments bring relief, some don't, but nothing offers a cure. Sometimes, in between flare-ups, I wonder if it's really as bad as I remember. During flare-ups, I wonder why my body is broken. It's difficult to have a condition where there's nothing to blame: no virus or bacteria, no fractured bone or torn muscle, and nothing that's visible in a test that I could show my friends and family.

However, some people believe that there is actually something specific to blame for fibromyalgia—Epstein-Barr Virus (EBV) to be exact. Anthony William refers to himself as the Medical Medium and insists that EBV (also known as mono) is responsible not only for fibromyalgia, but also chronic fatigue syndrome, thyroid disease, vertigo, and tinnitus.[253] William suggests a regimented diet centred around celery juice as the cure for undiagnosed EBV.[254] There is no scientific or medical evidence that celery juice is capable of treating EBV or can cure fibromyalgia.[255] There's also no scientific or medical evidence that EBV is being left undiagnosed in patients, or that it causes any of these conditions (or many others listed on William's website).[256]

This approach is common in the wellness industry, which frequently blames indescribable toxins for common symptoms that most people experience to some degree, such as fatigue, aches and pains, and lack of concentration. These toxins are indescribable for a reason: they don't exist. Bodies naturally filter out any substances that don't belong in them, so while it can make us feel nice to detox for a few days because we are focusing on our bodies and drinking juices, expensive wellness trends help the companies marketing them more than the people adopting them.[257] However, there are plenty of unmoderated anecdotes from people who have tried apple cider vinegar cleanses, activated charcoal smoothies, or celery juice diets, and share their promising results with the internet, thus encouraging more people to try it.

I was introduced to the Medical Medium by a meditation teacher and massage therapist, who told me people are "getting better" and there is a "cure" for fibromyalgia. "What have you got to lose?" he asked. I don't know whether he sincerely wanted to help me or was benefiting in some way by promoting celery juice to his clients but, either way, he is another example of a wellness practitioner taking advantage of other people's desperation.

I haven't started drinking celery juice and I don't believe that fibromyalgia has a cure—although I'm willing to be proven wrong by clinical studies. Despite placing my faith in medical research, I don't consider medical science to be infallible either. There is so much that science hasn't discovered yet and I know our medical system is guided by economic and political influences, rather than a moral imperative to improve public health.[258] I am still grappling with the daily frustration that comes from navigating the selfish motivations of pharmaceutical companies and wellness industry grifters, and the well-intentioned, but misinformed, guidance that can come from both medical doctors and holistic health practitioners, all while simply trying to manage my symptoms and reduce the number of days where my pain is too severe for me to get out of bed.

Sometimes having a chronic health condition can make you feel like you are completely helpless, so being told what to do next by somebody who claims to have a cure for your incurable illness can be extremely tempting. In fact, ignoring them might make it seem like you are instead choosing to wallow in your pain rather than saving yourself from a lifetime of chronic pain. Maybe you *want* to be sick. This temptation can lead people to spend years of their lives and thousands of dollars seeking unproven and untested treatments to cure the symptoms they are experiencing.

One controversial example of this is the diagnosis of chronic Lyme disease. Lyme disease is a tick-borne illness that was only discovered in 1975 after local children developed rashes and other symptoms in the town of Lyme, Connecticut.[259] The black-legged tick (or deer tick) can carry a bacteria called *borrelia burgdorferi* which can cause a bullseye rash, joint and muscle pain, fevers and chills, and swollen lymph nodes in humans upon exposure. This acute response was termed Lyme disease and can be treated with antibiotics.

Somewhere between 5% and 20% of patients with acute Lyme disease continue to experience symptoms like fatigue and brain fog after completing their antibiotics regimen, and are diagnosed with post-treatment Lyme disease syndrome, or PTLDS.[260] Medical science is less certain about what causes these symptoms; some physicians believe it is caused by the persistent presence of *borrelia burgdorferi* in a patient's system, while others believe that *borrelia burgdorferi* can cause an autoimmune response in some patients. Either way, the symptoms of PTLDS are documented and effective treatment unfortunately remains elusive, with clinical studies showing long-term courses of antibiotics perform no better to treat symptoms than placebos.

The controversy arises with the introduction of chronic Lyme disease, which is different to PTLDS and is not a condition recognised by medical science. Some doctors—referred to as Lyme-literate doctors by the chronic Lyme community—will ascribe this condition to patients if they have a range of symptoms, including muscle pain, fatigue, and anxiety.[259] A diagnosis of chronic Lyme disease does not require patients to present with any evidence of prior exposure to black-legged ticks or *borrelia burgdorferi* bacteria, which is the main reason it is classified separately to acute Lyme disease and PTLDS.[259]

But if patients have not been exposed to *borrelia burgdorferi*, why are they experiencing chronic and often debilitating symptoms? Some clinicians believe chronic Lyme patients have been misdiagnosed and likely have a different chronic illness.[260] However, the options tend to be other under-researched conditions that offer limited explanations and treatments, like fibromyalgia or chronic fatigue syndrome.[260] Other doctors dismiss chronic Lyme patients entirely, suggesting that they are overreacting to everyday aches and pains or making up their symptoms for attention.[260]

Almost everybody with a chronic health condition has had their symptoms dismissed or minimised by strangers, friends and family, or the medical system. Sometimes we diminish our own pain too, assuming we're just weak and it's not that bad. Once I had stomach cramps for three days and I dismissed them as my usual pain until they became so bad that I went to the hospital. Turns out I had a kidney infection. We dread going to new doctors because we're worried how they will respond to us explaining our medical history, and we downplay our symptoms to others to avoid their judgement. There's an entire forum dedicated to identifying individuals that people believe are faking their symptoms or conditions.[263] People trawl through and analyse social media posts and then publicly, and often cruelly, expose them for entertainment.

Throughout history, women have especially been subjected to others misunderstanding our illnesses, minimising our pain, and dismissing our symptoms.[264] Doctors have ignored women's genuine complaints for millennia in favour of using fake medical diagnoses like hysteria to institutionalise women who are deemed inconvenient or immoral. Some conditions, like fibromyalgia—which affects nine times more women than men—have only recently been recognised and are lacking the breadth of study into symptoms, causes, and treatments that more male-centric conditions have received.[265] People with fibromyalgia typically see a minimum of 10 specialists, and take an average of seven years, before they are diagnosed.[266] Other conditions like endometriosis have been underestimated for decades, with uterus-bearing individuals being turned away from emergency wards for period cramps despite the pain becoming so severe that it can cause patients to lose consciousness.[262]

When you're used to your symptoms being ignored or mocked by traditional pathways, it's not hard to understand why people are seeking a diagnosis like chronic Lyme disease—and significantly more women are treated for chronic Lyme than men.[262] Having this condition allows you to have access to Lyme-literate doctors who offer detailed treatment plans, an entire community of supportive people ready to embrace individuals and validate their experiences, and something tangible to blame for your ongoing chronic suffering: a pesky bacteria. Whether or not chronic Lyme is real is less relevant to these patients than the acceptance and community they have found with fellow chronic Lyme believers. There are many examples of other groups who have gathered together based on a shared belief, and who value the community that this belief provides. In some ways, it feels better to have a fake illness that comes with a community and treatment options than to have a real condition that leads to isolation and has no cure.

Due to the sense of community the diagnosis brings, chronic Lyme evolves for many people from a condition to an identity. This makes it especially difficult for sufferers to consider alternative ideas and solutions, because the prospect of losing that identity is too challenging.[264] We spend our entire lives seeking clarity and understanding, so if you think you have found it, it's scary to return to uncertainty and unknowns.

Perhaps it's fine to let patients continue to believe they have chronic Lyme if it is helping them find clarity and community. Placebo effects have been proven to genuinely help reduce symptoms like pain, insomnia, fatigue, and nausea. Even taking a placebo medication that you *know* is a placebo can still reduce symptoms more than doing nothing.[268] If individuals believe they have a condition and that the steps they are taking are treating that condition, it's possible they are able to make themselves feel better purely through this action. Provided the treatment they're choosing doesn't do further harm to themselves or others, it's not worth diminishing the benefits of a placebo for the sake of being *right*.

Unfortunately, diagnosing and treating chronic Lyme is not harmless. One of the main treatments for chronic Lyme is long courses of antibiotics, which has tangible risks. Overuse of antibiotics can create antimicrobial resistance and lead to more severe infections, as well as increase the risk of cardiovascular diseases, certain types of cancer, and premature death.[64,269] People are even told that negative reactions to treatments are a good sign, Chronic Lyme patients often believe that having adverse side effects to medication is a signal that the body is detoxifying and healing.[264] These symptoms are referred to as "herxing".[264]

Herxing is another name for the Jarisch-Herxheimer Reaction or JHR, which is a legitimate reaction to antibiotics that some patients experience during the treatment of bacteria-based illnesses. JHR is most commonly seen in the treatment of syphilis, but has also been identified in cases of Lyme disease, leptospirosis, and relapsing fever.[270] However, there is no evidence chronic Lyme is caused by the persistent presence of bacteria, and encouraging chronic Lyme patients to believe any negative side effects they experience are actually a positive indication of healing can cause people to ignore health risks.[264]

People have believed negative side effects are positive indicators for centuries. There are records of ancient Egyptians using laxatives for a range of conditions, presumably because there was evidence that at least *something* was happening as a result of taking them.[271] Similar logic was applied with American patent medicines in the 19th century, with many claiming that side effects like vomiting and diarrhoea were an indicator that the medication was working.[272] It was widely assumed that if a medication was having any effect, it was having a *positive* effect.

This same logic continues to be applied today, not just with chronic Lyme but with a range of wellness and biohacking products and treatments recommended by many companies and influencers. Side effects like vomiting and diarrhoea—as well as other indicators like fevers, stomach cramps, bloating, dehydration, and blood in the stool— are described as toxins leaving the body.[272] Advice offered by wellness influencers and biohacking tech bros is largely unregulated, meaning that anybody who feels that they have impurities to purge or inefficiencies to fix can partake in the variety of suggested treatments and potentially harm themselves in the process.[257]

It's not hard to sell solutions to people who have been seeking them for a long time. After years of searching for answers, I was quick to believe that my entire constellation of symptoms was explained by the alignment of my jaw and the length of my lingual frenulum. I remember holding my A4 page of notes and calling my mum from the dentist's carpark to tell her about the discovery, the next steps, and the potential for treatment. It's nice to find something to blame—especially when it's something external that can possibly be fixed through surgery or medication—because the alternative might be dealing with an untreatable condition or needing to do meaningful work to improve your mental health.

At a Lyme support group journalist Molly Fischer attended, she heard somebody say that it's important to remember that emotional or cognitive disorders can be the only visible symptoms of chronic Lyme disease, with possible manifestations including "depression, anxiety, irritability, rage, hyperactivity, and problems with attention and focus".[264] When chronic Lyme is used to explain conditions like anxiety and depression, it allows people to blame a tick and the bacteria it carries for their mental health challenges rather than needing to reckon with the idea that it's "all in your head". And I don't mean that as a way of dismissing the validity of those challenges—my mental health conditions are all in my head. So are the various pain and sensation problems that my fibromyalgia causes. My brain tries to process the signals that my nerves are communicating, and sometimes gets it wrong. But everything we perceive in this world is all in our heads; that doesn't make the pain we feel or the emotions we experience any less *real*.

Although science has deepened our understanding of the world in significant ways, it still cannot explain everything. Medical science has developed astronomically in the last couple of centuries in ways that we now take for granted, granting us access to vaccines, germ theory, essential vitamins, antibiotics, and organ transplants.[273] Scientists had no credible evidence that smoking was harmful until the mid-1950s, despite that seeming obvious to us now.[274]

Finding the limits of medical science can be devastating when you are suffering and searching for answers.[275] It can also be difficult for doctors to acknowledge these limits, and there's a fine line between being open-minded to the next scientific discovery and spreading false information based on speculation and hope.[264]

I think it's okay to exist in the unknown sometimes. We don't know what causes fibromyalgia yet, but the universe is full of inexplicable things. We have only classified about 9% of the ocean's species.[276] Researchers can't agree on the reasons we yawn.[277] The way gravity works is still not fully understood.[278] But less than 300 years ago, we also didn't know what caused thunder.[279] We desperately want something to explain the unexplainable, but sometimes we just need to wait for medicine and science to do its work (and, in the meantime, be grateful humans invented heat packs).

NEURODIVERSITY, MENTAL HEALTH, AND UNDERSTANDING OUR BRAINS

The human brain is extremely complex. It contains 86 billion neurons and—contrary to the pervasive myth that we only use approximately 10% of our thinking power—almost all of those nerve cells become active whenever we perform even the simplest of tasks.[280-282] However, our brains are also extremely adaptable. If our entire brain is available, we will make use of it, but we are also shockingly able to live a relatively normal life with only half of our brain intact.[283]

Human brains are unique in the animal kingdom. We are capable of a collection of actions, feelings, and beliefs other animals are not. Although some animals possess one or two abilities once considered uniquely human (self-recognition in a mirror, empathy for others, the use of tools, the ability to wage war),[284] no other creatures on Earth have been quite so effective at developing language, creating cultural artefacts, and advancing the scientific understanding of our universe.

In high school, we read textbooks that tell us the

uniqueness of human consciousness comes from the size and weight of our brains, the number of neurons they contain, and the amount of energy they use compared to our other processes and systems. However, anatomically, our brains behave almost exactly as we'd expect them to when we compare them to the brains of other primates.[280,284] That's what makes them remarkable: somehow, while our evolutionary ancestors are climbing trees (which, honestly, sounds quite nice), we are writing concertos.

Neuroscientists are using their formidable human intellects to understand how we can have this capacity when other animals do not. Preliminary theories suggest our brains are more "plastic"[282] and flexible than other primates, or different regions of our brains are more capable of communicating with each other and creating "synergies"[283] than other animals. But our brains continue to confound and confuse the people who study them, with some neuroscientists having started developing artificial intelligence that can be more effective than we are at identifying patterns in how we think.[287]

It amazes me that our brains—capable of so many things—are still unable to fully understand themselves. This is evident at the neuroscientific scale, but also in our day-to-day lives. Why can my brain be fully cognizant of its own limitations, challenges, and irrational feelings, but remain unable to reason with itself?

I often wish I could tell my brain to stop registering the pain signals it's receiving. Pain is an incredibly important cue—people with congenital insensitivity to pain (i.e. the inability to feel pain) can struggle to learn how their bodies exist in physical space and often collect an array of cuts, bruises, and bone fractures without realising.[288] Our bodies create the sensation of pain through a complicated process that requires accurate communication between nerve fibres, the spinal cord, and the brain, and congenital insensitivity to pain occurs when a rare genetic variation interrupts this communication.[289]

This game of telephone is also science's best guess for why I experience chronic pain.[254] My nervous system is still communicating with my brain, but it is often sending invalid or unhelpful signals that suggest I am in pain when my body is actually fine. These pain signals aren't important data—they're not helping me learn how to traverse my environment, avoid risks, or protect myself from harm. But despite rationally knowing that, my brain is unable to tell itself, "Hey, don't worry about that one; it's a false positive." Similarly, I have limited success reasoning with myself when I'm feeling unnecessarily anxious, having trouble concentrating, or am feeling overstimulated by perfectly normal things like the feeling of my clothing against my skin.

As I mentioned when I was celebrating the merits of potatoes, I've always been a selective eater. I have more dietary range now than I used to, but there are still many foods I can't eat, especially when I'm feeling particularly overstimulated or overwhelmed. Rice is a good example of this: I actively taught myself to enjoy rice in 2013 before I travelled to Japan, but there are still some days where the texture makes it near impossible for me to swallow.

On those days, I know objectively this is a perfectly safe and delicious food that billions of people eat every day, but I still can't persuade myself to eat it. The more I think about it, the harder it gets.

Throughout my childhood, most adults thought my inability to eat certain foods was a decision, as though I were being obstinate, exaggerating my reactions, and choosing to be a troublemaker. I understand my fussiness was an inconvenience—I imagine it was difficult for my parents to either cook multiple meals each night, eat the same thing repeatedly, or watch me struggle to force certain foods down one mouthful at a time. But I also can't imagine anybody *choosing* to be fussy.

I remember when I was thirteen on a school camp, I deliberately stayed in my tent and pretended to sleep through dinner because I knew I wouldn't be able to eat the meal being offered that night. There were many school lunches I gave to friends or threw in the bin because I couldn't eat them, but I was also too ashamed to bring them back home. I had so many feelings: I felt embarrassed because I was privileged enough to have access to food but I couldn't eat it, I felt guilty because I was wasting my parents' time and money, and I felt frustrated because other kids could eat anything and I wanted to do that too. I felt alone because I couldn't explain what I was experiencing to anyone else, at first because I was too young to articulate it, and then because shame is an incredible suppressant. And I felt *hungry*. No child would choose those feelings. No adult would, either.

Going to a new restaurant or visiting somebody

new for dinner still causes anxiety, especially when being forthcoming and explaining my selective eating can be risky. Despite being a (relatively) autonomous adult human being, fussiness is still often met with jokes at best and judgement at worst. And, to some extent, I understand it. If you've never experienced the complete inability to eat certain foods, it must seem ridiculous. And yet, just as some people cannot explain to their amygdala that public speaking is not worthy of an extreme fight or flight response, I am unable to use reason to eat foods on my brain's "no, thank you" list.

My brain is full of eccentricities like this one, but I'm not unique in that sense; all of us have our own assortment of nonsensical truths that we recognise with varying levels of awareness. Just as neuroscience is trying to understand the human brain overall, each of us spends our entire lives trying to untangle the specific feelings, desires, and irrationalities within our own minds. We may each have 86 billion neurons, but they all fire a little bit differently.

The differences between our brains is what makes our relationships with others so fascinating and infuriating. This diversity helps civilization function because each of us has varied competencies and interests, ensuring we are able to fill the discrete roles that are needed for society to continue and evolve. This is similar to how ecosystems operate: plants, animals, fungi, and bacteria are more likely to thrive and are less susceptible to disease in biodiverse environments than they are in monocultures.[290]

I'm not the first person to draw a parallel between heterogeneous ecosystems and heterogeneous ways of thinking. In 1998, Harvey Blume wrote that "neurodiversity may be every bit as crucial for the human race as biodiversity is for life in general".[291] This article was referenced in the honours thesis of Judy Singer, a sociologist who further popularised the term neurodiversity.[292] I suspect that neither Blume nor Singer anticipated the way this word would become part of the vernacular for people with neurological conditions, but it has since been adopted as a way to celebrate the unique qualities these conditions can bring, a means of empowerment, a type of identity, and a title for a social justice movement.[293]

The neurodiversity movement is dedicated to improving the rights of people who are considered neurodivergent. Some sources treat these two terms as synonymous; however, neurodiversity refers to the collective variety of human thinking, while neurodivergence (and neurodivergent people) specifically describes people who somehow deviate from the "cognitive norm".[293,294] An individual can be neurodivergent, but only a group can be neurodiverse.

Although neurodivergent is a relatively simple term to define, understanding which specific conditions, impairments, and phenotypes (i.e. observable traits) are considered non-typical is more challenging. This topic is contested between different sources, expanding or restricting the definition to include a varying number of developmental disabilities, nervous system conditions, learning impairments, mental health conditions, and brain injuries.[295]

The one area of consensus between almost every source is that autistic people are neurodivergent—presumably because terms like neurodiverse, neurodivergent, and neurotypical originate from discussions of autistic rights. In fact, some people treat neurodivergent and neurotypical as synonyms for autistic and allistic respectively. (Allistic simply means non-autistic. Having a specific term for this is important as it allows us to have conversations about people's behaviour and thought patterns without defining them based on whether they are autistic vs. not autistic or, worse, autistic vs. *normal.*)

While we're discussing language, this is a good time to mention that I have used both identity-first and person-first language while writing this book, despite my usual desire to follow grammatical rules with extreme consistency and rigour. People have different feelings about whether they prefer to use identity-first language (e.g. autistic person) or person-first language (e.g. person with autism) to describe themselves. The person-first movement began in 1974, with advocates wanting shorthand to express that people are more important than their conditions or disabilities, and they should be seen as humans above all else—that, literally, the person should come *first.*[296] But, as people develop vibrant communities around their identities, some have started pushing for their identities to come first again, as a way of demonstrating their self-acceptance and reducing stigma.[297] Personally, I'm not particularly passionate one way or the other, and generally choose based on the preference of the person I'm speaking to, or on which phrase sounds better in a sentence. I often lean towards identity-first language because it's less wordy, but for some conditions it's hard to find the adjective you need to make it work. (For example, I can't refer to myself as a *fibromyalgia person*. Fibromyalgic person? Fibromyalgian?)

The creation of new words and the debates around phrasing might seem trivial, but they're an important indicator that people with various disabilities, conditions, illnesses, and disorders are finally being given the space to decide together how they want to be treated. For example, many people in the Deaf community have been able to establish that they would like to be treated as a distinct cultural and linguistic minority, rather than a disabled group.[298] Similar discussions are happening in the autism rights movement, with advocates preferring to define autism as a difference rather than a disability.[292] A growing subset of research is encouraging medical practitioners to shift their focus away from the external presentations and supposed deficits of autism and instead consider the underlying causes and internal experiences of autistic people. In this model, autism is defined by difficulties processing sensory information, which can cause people to overreact and become hypersensitive to some stimuli while underreacting or being oblivious to others. However, autism—or autism spectrum disorder (ASD)—is still officially classified as a "developmental disability".[299] Current medical diagnostic criteria states that ASD is identified through external and observable traits, such as a person's challenges with communication, repetitive behaviours and interests, and non-typical ways of interacting with others and the world.[299]

The term autism was first used in 1911 by Eugene Bleuler, and referred to symptoms of severe schizophrenia rather than a standalone developmental condition, specifically to describe the hallucinations, fantasies, and "inner world"[300] of schizophrenic patients. Children who would be diagnosed with ASD today may have previously been diagnosed with childhood schizophrenia, due to an overlap in challenges like developing language and social skills.[301] Leo Kanner borrowed the term autism in 1943 to describe children who seemed to find it difficult to function outside of their inner world—not due to the fantasies described by Bleuler, but rather due to strict routines, specific interests, and the confusing nuances of interacting with others.[302] Kanner's seminal work eventually led to "infantile autism"[303] being officially listed as a separate diagnosis from schizophrenia in the DSM-III in 1980 (changing to "autistic disorder"[303] when the DSM-IIIR was published in 1987).

But Bleuler may not have been the only person Kanner was borrowing from. In 1944, on an entirely different continent, Hans Asperger published a paper describing children with similar traits using the same term: autism. Asperger studied patients across a wide range of ages and characteristics, including patients who were mute, who engaged in repetitive hand movements, or who talked obsessively about their specialised interests.[304] Despite their work sharing similar findings and using the same terms, Kanner's paper became a notable and influential work while Asperger's went relatively unnoticed at the time. However, this changed in 1981, when a child psychiatrist named Lorna Wing introduced Asperger's work to the English-speaking autism community as a way of arguing for an expanded diagnostic criteria for autism.[300]

Wing's endeavour was successful, and in 1994 the DSM-IV entry for autistic disorder expanded to include four subcategories, one of which is the well-known Asperger's disorder.[302] Asperger's was removed as a diagnosis from the DSM-5 in 2013, with all of the subcategories combined under the new autism spectrum disorder (ASD) instead. ASD was designed to be a compromise that allowed for more flexibility within the autism diagnosis while still acknowledging that autism can present in a myriad of ways: "with or without intellectual disability, with or without language impairment, and with severity levels ranging from 'requiring support' to 'requiring very substantial support'".[302] Removing Asperger's from the DSM led to debate within both research and advocacy communities, with people feeling as though it removed a level of specificity that they appreciated or that it erased an identity that some people had associated with for almost twenty years.[302]

Around the same time the DSM-5 was published, an investigative journalist named Steve Silberman released a book analysing the discoveries of Kanner and Asperger, as well as exploring the history of ASD more broadly.[305] Prior to Silberman's research, people assumed that the similarities between Kanner and Asperger's work were a remarkable coincidence, similar to Gottfried Leibniz and Isaac Newton discovering calculus around the same time independently of one another.[306] However, Silberman revealed there is more to the story.

Although Kanner has been credited as being first to use the word autism to describe the children he was researching, Siberman found Asperger was using this term for the same purpose in lectures as early as 1938, six years prior to the publication of his research and findings.[304] Silberman also found Kanner was undeniably aware of Asperger's earlier work; in 1938, George Frankl, the chief diagnostician at Asperger's clinic, moved from Vienna to Baltimore and began working in Kanner's clinic. Silberman argues Frankl shared Asperger's ideas and research with Kanner, who then produced his own paper in 1943 which became the foundational text for autism diagnosis.

Kanner's surface-level understanding of Asperger's work shows in some of the errors Kanner made in his paper. For example, Kanner believed that autism is something children developed due to cold and distant parenting, while Asperger felt autism was a congenital condition. Kanner also believed autism was only present in infants and young children, it was extremely rare (affecting approximately four in 10,000 people), and very easily quantified with specific diagnostic criteria. The proliferation of these beliefs—which Asperger did not share—led to many autistic people, who fell outside the parameters Kanner specified, being denied support for much longer than was necessary.

Don't feel too bad for Asperger, though. For decades, it was believed Asperger saved many autistic children from being considered irredeemable by the Nazi regime in Austria.[305] However, it was discovered by historians Herwig Czech and Edith Sheffer in 2018 that he was actually complicit in the Nazi childhood euthanasia program, recommending several children be sent to a facility called Am Spiegelgrund, where children were experimented on and killed.[305] Although he was not officially in the Nazi party, their files vouch for Asperger's loyalty, share his medical files, and note that he associated with leaders in Vienna's euthanasia program.

So, when you realise that the first person to use the word autism to describe children with social challenges and repetitive behaviours was either a Nazi sympathiser or a psychiatrist who stole research from a Nazi sympathiser, it makes sense that autistic people developed their own communities so they could better understand and advocate for their own neurological differences. Jim Sinclair, an autism rights activist who co-founded the Autism Network International in 1992, was an early proponent of the idea that autism was not a pathology, and did not need to be, but rather, that autistic people should be accepted, supported, and better understood.[308,309] A few years later, in 1996, the popular *Independent Living on the Autistic Spectrum* (InLv) email list started, allowing autistic people to connect and share with one another.[310] These messages, organisations, and communities led to what is now considered the autism rights movement.[308]

The autism rights movement argued that fewer resources should be directed towards "fixing" autistic people and they should instead be channelled into "accommodations, supports, resources, and research to improve the quality of life for autistic people and their families".[311] After two generations of autistic people being institutionalised, experimented on, and completely underestimated, the autism rights movement shifted attention away from the pathological aspects of ASD towards acknowledging the unique perspectives, skills, and culture that autistic people can contribute to society, especially when granted access and compassion.[308] This approach does not discount the challenges autistic people and their families can face, nor does it suggest ASD is only something to be celebrated and it can never present difficulties. Rather, the movement attempted to centralise supporting autistic people so they can live productive and fulfilling lives, rather than focusing research and funding towards identifying risk factors, developing cures, or finding ways to eradicate ASD altogether.

The autism rights movement always included more than just autistic people, with the Autism Network International and InLv community referring to people with ADHD, dyslexia, dyscalculia, and other conditions as "cousins"[312] who were welcome to participate in the spaces they were creating. However, to more explicitly include this range of neurodivergence, advocates have started using the label neurodiversity movement instead, adopting the term that was first popularised by Blume and Singer.[291,292] Although Singer's initial thesis was about autism, she mentioned similar communities were being established by people with Attention Deficit Hyperactivity Disorder (ADHD) and dyslexia, and shared that her goal was always to "draw attention to a wide variety of conditions".[292,293]

Still, there are debates about who is *allowed* to be supported by the neurodiversity movement and who is not. Some make the distinction that neurodivergence only describes people with conditions that are congenital rather than acquired later in life, meaning people with traumatic brain injuries or degenerative conditions like dementia would not be included.[295,316] Some sources list mental health conditions like depression and anxiety as neurodivergent, while others claim they should not be included because this could lead to people celebrating mental illness rather than treating it.[295] Some sources even question whether ADHD should be considered neurodivergent because it is not always a lifelong condition and can be treated with medication.[295]

While these debates are academically interesting, I would argue there doesn't need to be distinct criteria for who classifies as neurodivergent. If the categorisation feels right for somebody, and the term helps them understand themselves, access support, or find community, then they should be allowed to use it. I feel similarly about the queer community; while some people try to gatekeep who is and isn't *allowed* to call themselves queer, I feel that another person using the label has very little impact on my life.

I think we— as much as we can while staying safe—should be opening the doors to our communities to anyone who might benefit from being in them because visibility, support, and access to knowledge helps improve everyone's ability to understand themselves. It took me ages to figure out I was bisexual, despite having crushes on both boys and girls throughout school, because bisexuality just wasn't visible to me. I remember when I was about fifteen, I became seriously concerned I was the wrong gender because women were supposed to like men and men were supposed to like women, but I liked both, so was I not a real girl? Even when I finally learnt about the differences between sexuality and gender, it still took more than a year for me to progress from "I wish I was bisexual so I could date women" to "Wait, I think the fact that I want to date women means I *am* bisexual."

There is a misconception that people pretend to be neurodivergent or queer (or both) because these labels are somehow *trendy* or *cool*, but in reality it's a challenging existence that offers more discrimination than social clout. I struggle to believe many people are pretending to have these identities for attention, and I'm not the only person with that belief.[313] Preventing people from participating in these communities due to arbitrary rules about cognitive conditions, sexualities, or genders we have only started understanding in the last century sounds unnecessarily exhausting.

In advocacy movements, exclusionary arguments about identity politics often come from the inside. For example, gender critical feminists (also known as trans-exclusionary radical feminists or TERFs) believe feminism should not advocate for trans women, while asexual and aromantic people often feel excluded from queer spaces because of comments other queer people make about ace/

aro identities.[314,315] However, contrary to the norm, gatekeeping in the neurodiversity movement seems to predominantly come from *outside* neurodivergent communities.

One researcher claims the neurodiversity movement dismisses the uniqueness of all of our minds and excludes people by dividing people into a neurodivergent in-group and a neurotypical out-group, but simultaneously complains that the boundaries of these groups are "not transparent or well-defined"[316] so it's hard for people to understand where they belong. Other researchers falsely claim proponents of neurodiversity are somehow banning autistic people from seeking the support they need because they believe autism is not a disability, despite neurodiversity advocates openly agreeing ASD can be debilitating for many people with the diagnosis, and that people should seek the support they want or need.[317,318] However, the wildest corner of the internet I found while doing this research was the blog of Dr. Manuel Casanova.

Casanova is a neurologist who has published several books about autism. He also maintains a blog called *Cortical Chauvinism* (I wish I was kidding) where he shares his strong opinions about the neurodiversity movement. He claims the neurodiversity movement cannot be trusted because it relies primarily on autobiographical accounts.[319] I feel this is a failure to recognise that the value of the movement is precisely that it allows people to speak on their own behalf. Casanova counters this by claiming the neurodiversity movement doesn't really allow neurodivergent people to speak for themselves because this "social club"[317] is comprised of neurotypical people pretending to be neurodivergent, who are working with an "autistic elite"[317] who do not represent the majority of autistic people.[320] Casanova's evidence for this claim is that "the majority of autistic individuals exhibit language/communication impairments"[317] and therefore most neurodivergent people physically cannot advocate for themselves.

There are many ways Casanova's arguments do not hold up to scrutiny. Notably, by conflating neurodivergence and autism, Casanova is discounting the number of people with different conditions who are also advocating for themselves through the neurodiversity movement. Putting this aside, Casanova misrepresents the number of autistic people who are impaired to the extent that they cannot speak on their own behalf. Somewhere between 25% and 50% of autistic children are nonverbal, meaning that they do not express themselves or articulate their thoughts verbally by approximately two years old.[321,322] But the label nonverbal can mean many things. It may mean a child can still understand language, even if they don't speak. Nonverbal children may still be able to respond to others with body language, gestures, and sounds.[321] Some nonverbal children are able to learn speech later in their childhood and even into adolescence.[323] For others, their speech remains limited, but they can use other communication methods like sign language, writing, or typing.

This is one of the reasons online communities like InLv became invaluable to autistic people in the mid-1990s. For autistic people who could not verbally communicate or who sometimes found the experience of expressing themselves aloud frustrating, typing to other autistic people in forums and mailing lists became an outlet.[310] Philip Reyes, a nonverbal autistic boy, writes a blog to share his experiences and answer questions from readers.[320] The internet allows him to engage with the world in a way that he would not be able to otherwise. Philip is incredibly articulate and capable of expressing his experiences and desires via text, so Casanova may consider him part of his autistic elite despite the fact that Philip was unable to understand basic sentences or use the toilet independently when he was nine years old.

This isn't to say there aren't autistic people who cannot communicate their needs—as well as some who do not know their needs well enough to communicate them in the first place—but who is to say that neurotypical people are more capable of advocating for those individuals than other neurodivergent people? Casanova claims the neurodiversity movement is biased, but he fails to see his own bias in his writing. By referring to people with ASD who require more support as "the ones at the bottom"[319] or stating that the neurodiversity movement appeals to the "imagination"[319] and is an "escape from reality",[319] Casanova demonstrates that he thinks neurodivergent people are not truly equal to neurotypical people. Perhaps, even more personally, that autistic people are lesser than *him*.

Regardless of the definition of neurodivergent that we are using, there's a pervasive attitude that the term is synonymous with *lesser*. This leads to stigma, which can cause people to remain purposefully ignorant of the traits they see in themselves or their children, or try to avoid sharing their challenges and needs with others, or refuse to seek diagnosis or treatment for a condition. The assumption that having a cognitive condition, learning disorder, or mental illness should be marked by shame or pity is one of the concepts that neurodiversity advocates are attempting to challenge.

I've personally experienced this. When I first suspected I was neurodivergent and decided to get tested by a psychologist, I mentioned it to a friend. They responded like I was telling them I suspected I had a terminal illness, apologising for some perceived loss. But when I was diagnosed with both ASD and ADHD, I actually didn't lose anything—I actually gained a better understanding of my brain and some of the behaviours I've always had, social cues I've struggled with, and habits I used to be embarrassed by.

I think some people believe that a diagnosis, or *label*, is something that confines us; their apology implies that we were free but are now trapped. But this isn't how I feel at all. I was confined by the expectations placed on me—by society and by myself—far more than I am by this self-awareness I've been granted. I know this isn't an experience shared by everyone, but for me, finding an explanation for how my brain processes the world was not a cage—it was a key. It has granted me permission to stop restricting my behaviour and allow myself to be a more unbridled version of myself. It allowed me to fully embrace my periods of hyperfocus, to find ways to switch between tasks more successfully, and to express my needs to others rather than always adapting my behaviour to suit the preferences of the people around me. I still have a lot to discover, but learning I have ASD and ADHD is not something anybody needs to be *sorry* for. It's simply information that can help me interact with other people and the world.

The stigma around neurodivergence is dissolving somewhat, due to those same online communities that helped neurodivergent people find one another in the 1990s.[310] Increased visibility of conditions like ASD and ADHD through social media has led to more people identifying with their phenotypes rather than being ashamed of them, especially teenagers and young adults.[324] Dr Adeola Adelayo, a child and adolescent psychiatrist, believes this increased visibility and sense of community has led to young people having a much better understanding of their mental health than previous generations. Dr Adelayo specifically notes children and teenagers are more likely to seek treatment for anxiety conditions, with increased awareness and the reduction in social stigma making it easier for them to recognise the signs and feel comfortable raising them to a trusted adult.

Anxiety is the most common mental illness in Australia for people aged between 16 and 85, with 1 in 6 (17%) Australians currently diagnosed with some form of anxiety condition.[325] As such, it's also one of the most commonly self-diagnosed conditions, with people noticing symptoms like "panic attacks, palpitations, shaking, insomnia, and constant worry"[324], and using internet research or their own prior knowledge of those symptoms to infer they have anxiety.[324] With this knowledge, they are able to more easily manage their condition, seek treatment, or have an informed conversation with a health professional.

There are other conditions and symptoms people are also able to self-diagnose quite effectively. For example, middle-aged cis women are good at accurately self-diagnosing menopause and perimenopause.[324] People are able to identify changes in moles on their skin or lumps in their breasts that could be an early indicator of cancer, and can identify when they're feeling fatigued all the time and will often request a blood test to check for conditions like anaemia.[324] Self-diagnosing like this can be surprisingly beneficial, with studies showing that patients who research potential conditions can have more mutually beneficial conversations with their health professionals, find it easier to understand a diagnosis and have opinions about treatment options, ask more thorough questions, make the most of time-limited appointments, and experience faster diagnosis and treatment periods.[326-328] For example, it was easier for me to finally get my fibromyalgia diagnosis because I had a suspicion when I visited my doctor in 2020 and I had read the diagnostic criteria before I arrived at my appointment.

Increasing the speed of diagnosis and treatment and minimising the number of appointments it takes for a patient to get there has obvious benefits: it ensures a patient is able to receive relief from their symptoms sooner and more conveniently. It also allows greater access to healthcare for people for whom appointments and wait times are prohibitively expensive, or who find it difficult to attend appointments due to factors like their age or accessibility needs.[327] It can also reduce the pressure on our medical system overall, giving everybody trying to access healthcare a better experience.[327]

There are some concerns with self-diagnosis, however. Online sources are not necessarily written or reviewed by medical professionals, and so if somebody is not research literate they might be reading incorrect information.[326] Even if the information is accurate, it might lead a person to consider their symptoms with more or less urgency than required, to become unnecessarily worried about their potential condition, or to become so fixated on a particular diagnosis that they are close-minded to other possibilities.[326,327] Online research can also lead people to pursue treatments that aren't beneficial or could be harmful, or that should not be undergone without medical supervision.[328] But when coupled with conversations with health professionals, researching our conditions and understanding them more effectively allows us to have agency in our healthcare—which is something that many marginalised people have been denied for most of history.[329,330]

When my psychologist told me she suspected I had ASD and ADHD, she set me several tests to complete. When I returned home from my appointment, I started researching those diagnostic tools and reading medical journals similar to those I sought out when I was first trying to understand fibromyalgia. The first test of those was the Autism Spectrum Quotient (AQ-50), which was published in 2001 and originally designed to be a "self-administered instrument"[329] for adults without learning disabilities to measure whether they had autistic traits. The purpose of the AQ-50 was to fill a gap the authors saw in diagnostic processes at the time: giving individuals without significant learning difficulties the ability to independently check whether their challenges and behaviours might classify them as autistic *before* seeking additional support.[329]

The original paper actually states that the tool was made for "adults of normal intelligence"[331] to assess where they are on a scale of "autistic to normality".[331] However, I—along with neurodiversity advocates—believe we should steer away from referring to atypical or minority traits as *abnormal* traits, especially when these are naturally occurring variations of human thought and expression. As a society, we make assumptions about different behaviours and place value judgements on them, often without questioning it.[293] For example, we assume if a person is fidgeting or not making eye contact, they are not listening. During a lecture, somebody might learn better while moving around the space, but our social norms dictate that they should be stationary. Social conventions, expectations, and morals are vital for our society to remain functional overall. However, it is equally important to question our implicit biases to ensure we are not creating unpleasant experiences for some people entirely unnecessarily, simply by deeming their behaviours abnormal simply because they are atypical.

The original recommendation from the creators of the AQ-50 is that if a person scores higher than 32 on the test and is experiencing some sort of "distress"[329] or challenge as a result of their autistic traits, then they likely have ASD, and should therefore be referred to a clinician for a full diagnostic assessment. A 2005 analysis of the tool suggested people can actually score much lower than 32 on the AQ-50 and still be autistic, but that this high cutoff was chosen to reduce the risk of false positives when the tool is used as a self-diagnostic instrument in the general population.[332] Ultimately, a person's score on the AQ-50 is less relevant than the ways their autistic traits impact their life, which can fluctuate depending on whether the people in their life accommodate the behaviours and preferences that may be seen as *abnormal* to others. This idea relates to the social model of disability, which essentially claims that people are not disabled by their bodies or minds, but rather by the ways society is built to accommodate some bodies and minds over others.[333] With this model, we can say that a person using a wheelchair is disabled by whether or not a building has a ramp or elevator, not by the physical condition that causes them to use a mobility aid. By applying this model, we can see that two individuals with the same AQ-50 scores might have very different experiences of the world based on environmental factors, such as the way they are treated by friends and family or how they are valued at work.[332] This experience is a greater signifier of whether somebody is diagnosed with ASD than their AQ-50 score alone.

Diagnosis is sometimes treated as an entirely objective process. However, it is heavily influenced by a person's personal situation and upbringing, the beliefs and knowledge of medical practitioners, the progression of scientific discovery, and a range of social and political factors. The Diagnostic and Statistical Manual has only been published for approximately 70 years, and the ever-changing nature of its contents (and the way those changes are influenced by sociopolitical factors) show that diagnoses are constructions created by fallible humans who are simply trying to improve our understanding of the world and our place in it.[316] Diagnoses are incredibly useful, but they are not static.

As a strange analogy, imagine that in the mid-1900s a scientist decided all plants with pink flowers were part of a new category that they called "pretty flowers". However, in the early 2000s, some new research determined that yellow flowers should also be part of the "pretty flowers" classification, causing the number of "pretty flowers" in the world to suddenly grow significantly larger, despite the fact that no new flowers were actually introduced. This is similar to the phenomena that is occurring with conditions like ASD. As we learn more about neurodivergence and expand the diagnostic criteria of different conditions, we allow more people to feel understood and access the support they need. The number of people who need those accommodations isn't necessarily increasing, we're just getting better at finding them.

This assertion is backed by evidence. A 2013 study looked for "clusters"[332] of children with autism and found that these clusters are more likely to be situated where there is greater access to diagnostic and treatment services. Similar statistics are revealed when looking at autism rates globally: higher rates of autism in children tend to be found in countries with a larger number of diagnostic and treatment services.[332] It is not because autism is more common in these countries, but rather because it is easier to be diagnosed there. In 2011, a study in South Korea found that the prevalence of autism in children was higher than in the United States despite previously being considered significantly lower; the reason cited was simply that approximately two thirds of the cases had been previously undiagnosed.[334]

When diagnostic criteria changes or expands for a particular condition, so does the rate that the condition appears in the population.[335] However, this isn't necessarily due to more people developing the condition. Rather, ASD is now being recognised in people who already had it. This shifting reality means we would be better served by directing funding towards improved outcomes and quality of life for autistic people, rather than towards studies focused on finding the cause of ASD in the population.

Humans are inherently curious, but our search to understand *why* people have certain conditions can cause harm. In 1998, Andrew Wakefield published a paper in the Lancet claiming autistic traits appeared in children after receiving the MMR (Measles, Mumps, Rubella) triad vaccine, following a test he conducted on a sample of eight children.[336] In 2005, the Lancet found evidence that Wakefield's original findings were marred by "severe research misconduct, conflict of interests, and probably falsehood"[334] and retracted the paper. The link between the MMR vaccine and autism has since been discredited by dozens of studies. But in those seven years, the damage was done: outlets like The Guardian, The New York Times, and The Washington Post interviewed devastated parents, news stories speculated whether celebrities were choosing to vaccinate their children, and lawyers in the United Kingdom and United States launched class action lawsuits against vaccine manufacturers.[334] "Vaccines cause autism"[337] became a prevailing myth and immunisation rates still haven't fully recovered. Ultimately, Wakefield's research brought us no closer to understanding the cause of ASD, but it did lead to a resurgence in measles, a disease that was previously considered eliminated in many countries thanks to vaccinations.[338] Wakefield has doubled down on his position and continues to promote anti-vaxx ideas, most notably through his conspiratorial films *Vaxxed: From Cover-Up to Catastrophe* (2016) and *Vaxxed II: The People's Truth* (2019), which claim the Centers for Disease Control and Prevention (CDC) are deliberately covering up the link between vaccinations and autism.[337]

Research into the causes of ASD continues, although the focus has shifted from external factors to internal ones: genetics. Hundreds of genes have been identified as contributing to the difficulties with "communication, social cognition, and behaviour"[339] associated with ASD and it is believed that somewhere between 400 and 1,000 genes might be involved.[340] Simon Baron-Cohen—a leading ASD researcher working in the Autism

Research Centre in Cambridge, UK—believes that understanding the genetic causes of autism inherently "contributes to human knowledge",[340] but that there are also more practical benefits. He states that early identification of autism through genetic testing might allow people to be given better support as children as it would enable treatment of common comorbidities like epilepsy or gastrointestinal issues, allow intervention to support young autistic people who are at higher risk of developing mental health issues in their teenage years, and improve educational outcomes by providing accommodations earlier. While these are noble goals, not all researchers share them.

Many autistic people are sceptical of genetic research into the causes of ASD, fearing such research is aimed towards finding a *cure* for the condition or eradicating it through prenatal screening—a goal that some researchers have historically expressed in their consent forms.[341] Simon Baron-Cohen has been met with this scepticism firsthand, as he is one of the minds behind the Spectrum 10K study. Spectrum 10K was designed to be "the largest study of autism in the UK"[342] and aims "to investigate genetic and environmental factors that contribute to the wellbeing of autistic individuals and their families".[342] The study launched in August 2021 and immediately faced backlash from the autistic community, before being paused a month later for additional ethics assessments and consultation.[343] Additional methods for consultation with the autistic community were opened in 2023 before the study continues.[342]

When asked about whether the genetic findings of this study might contribute to goals like eradicating autism through genetic engineering and prenatal screening, Baron-Cohen expressed that he would be "horrified at this application of science".[340] However, his genetic research—and the research of scientists like him—can still inadvertently benefit scientists who undervalue autistic people and believe the condition should be cured or eradicated.[344] Current structures for genetic research often aren't compliant with UNESCO's 1997 Universal Declaration on the Human Genome and Human Rights.[344] Genetic data isn't always appropriately anonymised, researchers are granted access to genetic databases without participants receiving consent forms for each new study they are being included in, and researchers often do not involve disabled social scientists in the development of their research projects.[344]

It would not be the first time a genetics researcher had their findings applied in a way that "horrified"[345] them. In 1959, Jérôme Lejeune was the first author on a paper that described the genetic cause of Down Syndrome (also known as trisomy 21, due to it occuring when a person has an extra copy of chromosome 21).[345] Prior to this discovery, there was a widely held public belief that Down Syndrome was associated with race or with irresponsible parenting.[345] Supposedly, Lejeune was drawn to this research because he felt great compassion for children with the condition and their families, and wanted to find a way to treat its symptoms. However, after the publication of his paper, other researchers, scientists, and medical practitioners began to advocate for the use of this discovery to prenatally screen for Down Syndrome.[345]

Prenatal screening was initially used to identify conditions and malformations that would put the life of the baby, the carrier, or both at risk.[346] In situations where this was confirmed, parents would sometimes opt to terminate the pregnancy.[346] When prenatal screening was expanded to include non-life-threatening conditions like trisomy 21, the decision was often the same. The plummeting rates of Down Syndrome present in children has been referred to as a form of modern eugenics.[344] Between the 1980s and 2000s, the number of Down Syndrome cases diagnosed prenatally in Australia increased from 3% to 60% in mothers under 35.[347] Of those cases, only 5.3% were not terminated. Similar rates have been reported in the United Kingdom and parts of Europe. This is likely due to several factors, including the increased financial and emotional burden of raising a disabled child, the perception of that child's (and the parents') potential quality of life, and societal stigma leading to the devaluation of disabled people in general.[347]

Lejeune was appalled that his work was used to prenatally screen for, and often terminate, pregnancies where trisomy 21 was evident.[345] He was a staunchly pro-life Catholic who believed pregnancies should be carried to term under all circumstances.[345] He also disagreed with abortions that were carried out to protect the life or health of the carrier.[345] While I disagree with his anti-choice stance, Lejeune is a clear example that the intentions and desires of a researcher do nothing to influence the applications of their research.

It's also worth noting that, although Lejeune has received much of the credit for the discovery of trisomy 21, there is growing evidence the discovery was predominantly due to the experimental work of Marthe Gautier, a woman who worked alongside Lejeune in a lab run by Professor Raymond Turpin. In her testing, Gautier says she discovered that a person with Down Syndrome had an extra chromosome but her equipment was unable to identify which chromosome was duplicated. She "naively"[348] trusted Lejeune to photograph the slides on his equipment and only learned what he discovered six months later when she found out a paper was about to be published with his findings. The paper listed Lejeune as first author, Gautier as second, and Turpin as third—misspelling Gautier's name for good measure.

Later in her life, Gautier spoke out about the sexism in scientific research that she experienced throughout her career. She received a medal for her contributions to genetic research when she was 88, but was not permitted to accept the medal in a large ceremony or share her experiences with an audience because the Jérôme Lejeune Foundation sent two bailiffs to record Gautier's speech out of suspicion that it would tarnish Lejeune's memory.[348] When researchers have limited power over how their research is shared and applied, whether their research is correctly attributed, and whether they can speak about their experiences working in scientific fields, it's no wonder autistic people are sceptical about contributing to ongoing research into the causes of neurodivergence.

Still, Simon Baron-Cohen—who urges autistic people to participate in genetic research—and his many colleagues continue to contribute a wealth of research to the field. In fact, the AQ-50 test that I was asked to complete by my psychologist was developed by Baron-Cohen and his team at the Autism Research Centre. The AQ-50 was specifically designed to "catch"[332] more undiagnosed autistic people and allow them to access accommodations and support. The accessibility of this test—and similar screening tools, like the Social Responsiveness Scale for adults (SRS-A)—allows more people to explore their potential neurodivergence in their own time, minimising barriers and reducing stigma. They facilitate more open conversations between individuals and their partners, friends, and medical practitioners, overall leading to the normalisation of neurodiversity.[332]

Each of these screening tools are a little different. The AQ-50 is unique in that it measures a person's attention to detail and ability to imagine, while the SRS-A assesses for "social motivation"[349] instead. While both tests have been proven to be more effective at predicting ASD diagnosis in individuals than pure chance, the AQ-50 has been found to be more reliable overall.[349]

However, the AQ-50 is not without criticism. Baron-Cohen is one of the primary voices responsible for perpetuating the idea that all autistic people "lack a theory of mind",[350] are unable to meaningfully use their imagination or fantasise due to alexithymia, and are more likely to resonate with numbers and mathematics than language and arts.[351,352] His early research in these areas is reflected in the AQ-50, which asks questions such as "If I try to imagine something, I find it very easy to create a picture in my mind"[331], "I am fascinated by numbers"[331], and "I don't particularly enjoy reading fiction"[331] to assess whether somebody has ASD.

However, further research has shown that the assumption that all children with ASD lack a theory of mind is incorrect, as is the belief that this is a unique trait for children *with* ASD.[353] Findings that have been shared for nearly twenty years stating autistic people have "minds wired for science"[352] is also not a universal experience. The problem is that by integrating these findings into a test widely used to diagnose ASD, it becomes a self-fulfilling prophecy. The people who score high enough on the AQ-50 to receive an ASD diagnosis have to fit this model, and therefore further research conducted on people with a diagnosis reinforces the model while ignoring autistic people missed by the current criteria.

Our current practises around diagnosis for ASD and other neurodivergence is flavoured by the biases and subjectivity of researchers and medical practitioners. A person's background, upbringing, environment, stress levels, other illnesses, and previous traumas can all increase or decrease scores, causing them to be potentially misinterpreted if they are treated as objective and definitive diagnostic assessments.[354] After considering my AQ-50 score and the environmental factors that may have influenced it, my psychologist asked me to also complete a second test called the Camouflaging Autistic Traits Questionnaire CAT-Q.

This assessment was created in 2019 to measure "social-camouflaging"[355] behaviours (also known as masking). Autistic people use these techniques to disguise their autistic traits during social situations, and this can also influence how a person scores on other ASD tests.[355] My CAT-Q results showed that I had more masking behaviours than 91% of people my age.

This isn't surprising. It's been found that women with ASD are more likely to exhibit social-camouflaging behaviours than men.[356] It's theorised that the social expectations placed upon girls and women mean we are more likely to either become skilled actors by observing and imitating our peers, or to rely on being passive and shy to avoid inadvertently breaking social norms.[35,3587] Our ability to hide our ASD may be a contributing factor to why girls have significantly lower diagnosis rates than boys.[359]

Autism has historically been considered a male condition and, until relatively recently, it was thought that ASD only affected approximately one girl for every ten boys (1:10).[360,361] This has changed over the last five years, with the accepted ratio now closer to 1:3, and some neuroscientists believe the difference will reduce even further.[361] In addition to our tendency to mask our autistic traits, girls are also more difficult to diagnose because autistic diagnostic criteria were predominantly modelled on boys.[362] Our ASD tends to manifest in internal behaviours (e.g. low self-esteem, anxiety, depression, eating disorders, and self-harm) rather than external presentations (e.g. anger, aggression, behavioural problems, and inattention).[360] Some medical practitioners even have the preconceived idea that girls never have ASD and turn girls away or misdiagnose them with other conditions.[362] Studies have shown that even when boys and girls do present a similar level of autistic traits, girls typically need to either have significantly more behavioural problems, intellectual impairments, or both to be successfully diagnosed with ASD, due to the current biases of diagnostic criteria and medical practitioners.[362]

But prominent researchers like Baron-Cohen still perpetuate the idea that ASD is a male condition, even referring to it as a presentation of the "extreme male brain".[363] He argues there are two types of brain: a male type that is systematic and analytical, and a female type that is empathetic and compassionate.[350] He determined this by creating a test that assessed a person's capacity for empathy, and finding that women were likely to score higher on that test than men.[350] However, in his book *The Essential Difference*, he also states a person's gender does not dictate whether they have a male (systemising) or female (empathising) brain type.[350] Which raises the question: why do they need to have gendered names at all? This same question has been asked by neuroscientist Gina Rippon, whose work emphasises that cultural phenomena like Baron-Cohen's gender essentialism is the reason stereotypical understandings of gender continue to influence our medical practice and broader society.[364]

Rippon states that using innovative techniques to examine the brains of newborns has found that essential, biological gender differences are nonexistent.[364,365] There is a long history of "innumeracy, misinterpretation, publication bias, weak statistical power, inadequate controls, and worse"[366] in the study of gender and neuroscience, which has led to myths that now must be corrected through ongoing research. For example, a 2008 meta-analysis found language-processing is not more evenly spread across brain hemispheres in women than in men, and therefore there are no biologically innate differences in how different genders communicate.[366] It's also been found that certain features considered to be biological distinctions between men and women—like the percentage of grey to white matter—simply scale differently with overall brain size.[366] Neuroplasticity is a relatively new field of study that describes our brains' ability to adapt based on our experiences.[367] Furthermore, neuroscience is discovering that the differences between genders found in the study of adults are likely due to our brains being influenced through exposure to the stereotypes and messaging of a gendered world, rather than any innate biological reason.[364,365]

However, Baron-Cohen disagrees and is invested in proving there are biological distinctions that can explain how men and women perceive the world—not just social or cultural ones. He has conducted studies on where newborns gaze in their first twenty-four hours based on their gender, and on how the testosterone levels of amniotic fluid influence a person's brain as they age, but the results of this research is yet to be independently replicated.[368] Rippon has referred to this preoccupation as "neurotrash",[369] while fellow

neuroscientist Lise Eliot calls it "neurosexism".[366]
Baron-Cohen responded by writing a book review
in *The Psychologist*, telling these researchers the
biggest weakness in their arguments "is the
mistaken blurring of science with politics".[370]
(Watching scientific arguments occur over years
through published books, scholarly articles, and
book reviews is kind of wild.)

What Baron-Cohen seemingly fails to
understand in this defence of his research is that
science and politics are inherently connected.
The biases of researchers like him—whether they
are subconscious or explicit—make it harder for
autistic women to be understood and diagnosed,
which has an ongoing impact on the lives of
people like me. Stereotypes about how ASD
presents, coupled with the societal expectations
placed on young girls and the belief girls are less
likely to have ASD, means we are more likely to
have our ASD missed by parents, teachers, and
psychologists. This isn't just theoretical; this is
political.

For example, special interests can present
differently in girls. Special interests are the areas
that fascinate an autistic person, causing them to
become obsessed with researching, categorising,
and talking about that topic. Autistic boys tend to
be interested in things like "vehicles, computers,
or physics",[360] so these areas are often given as
examples during the diagnostic process; this can
cause girls—and their parents—to inadvertently
misrepresent their special interests to medical
practitioners.[360] However, autistic girls also have
special interests, they can just be more difficult

to spot. One theory is autistic girls often develop similar interests to others in their age group due to their tendency towards mimicry, so it's more difficult for parents and teachers to notice.[360] However, they obsess over these interests with a far greater depth and intensity to their allistic peers.[371] Another reason the special interests of autistic girls might remain under the radar is that they internalise these interests, preferring to spend time collecting and cataloguing information for themselves (which is definitely not how *literally this book* started) than speaking at length about the topic to others and drawing attention to it.[360,371]

There are some bizarre misunderstandings of how special interests are exhibited in general, likely due to how this trait is represented in the media. I found one incredible example of these misconceptions while exploring the rabbit hole of retrospective diagnosing—a field where people posthumously claim certain historical figures were neurodivergent based on their publications, diary entries, and descriptions from their peers. One example is Henry Cavendish, the philosopher and scientist who discovered hydrogen in the 1700s, who several researchers believe had ASD based on the way his contemporaries described his personality.[372] (It's hard not to be bitter that it seems easier for a dead man to receive an autism diagnosis in the early 2000s than it is for a living woman.)

In my reading, I quickly realised I was less confused by the arguments that Cavendish had ASD than I was by the arguments that he *didn't*. For example, Dr Fred Volkmar believes, although

Cavendish was "peculiar"[373] and "taciturn",[373] he is unlikely to have had ASD because he made significant discoveries during his lifetime, while autistic people generally "engage in an endless acquisition of facts, without doing anything productive"[373] because their condition makes them unable to reach "any sort of real accomplishment".[373] The idea that autistic people collect information on their special interests without ever turning it into something tangible is ignorant at best and ableist at worst. This perspective is even more alarming when you discover Volkmar was the primary author of the "Autism and Pervasive Developmental Disorders" section in the DSM-IV.[374] When the medical practitioners in charge of writing diagnostic standards have biases and misconceptions about neurodivergence, it's obvious why these permeate the medical system and society more broadly.

It's becoming more likely that the higher diagnosis rate of ASD in boys isn't due to an innate biological or genetic distinction. Rather, girls are being overlooked by current diagnostic standards and procedures.[359] There has been a push for diagnostic processes to be improved, especially to expand the criteria for ASD so girls are less likely to fall through the cracks. One paper proposes that traits like variations in special interests should be added to an official "female autistic phenotype" (which has the really unfortunate acronym FAP)[360] to help support medical practitioners in identifying and diagnosing girls with ASD.

Girls face remarkably similar diagnostic challenges with ADHD. As with ASD, ADHD is generally considered to be a condition that predominantly affects boys, which is likely due to the ADHD diagnostic criteria being created based on studies performed on "hyperactive white boys"[375] in the 1970s. ADHD was first described by Sir George Frederic Still (who has a fantastic name for somebody researching children who struggle to stop moving). He identified children deemed more impulsive and inattentive than the average child, while still being otherwise healthy.[376] His ideas were further researched in 1932, when German doctors Franz Kramer and Hans Pollnow observed "hyperkinetic"[376] reactions in children, which they described as a condition where children couldn't sit still and had trouble following rules. When the condition was first included in the DSM in 1968, the term hyperkinetic was used. It was changed to ADD in 1980 and ADHD in 1987.

In 2013, the DSM was updated to recognise that ADHD also affects adults, not just children, and lists three different "presentations"[238,377] of ADHD. This means that researchers have now determined that this same condition can appear in different ways for different people.[376] This is pertinent to our improved understanding of how ADHD impacts girls, as recent studies are finding that, on average, ADHD has different presentations and onset timelines in girls than boys.[375,378-380] However, even as our understanding of ADHD improves and diagnostic criteria expands, old knowledge and existing biases in the field mean medical practitioners are primed to overlook girls who present with ADHD symptoms, and often end up misdiagnosing them.[381,382]

Some of the differences between how ADHD

presents in girls and boys have direct parallels to ASD. For example, girls are more likely to use "compensatory strategies"[379] to mask their ADHD, similar to the social camouflaging used by autistic girls. Also, girls with ADHD tend to internalise their challenges, resulting in higher rates of depression and anxiety, as opposed to boys, who externalise their frustrations in disruptive or aggressive behaviours.[378-380] Similar to autism, the ways girls subconsciously hide and internalise their ADHD can lead to reduced rates of diagnosis, culminating in boys being three times more likely to receive an ADHD diagnosis than girls in childhood despite the rates of ADHD in adult men and women being almost equal.[379,380]

The difference in the rates of diagnosis in different age groups may, in part, be due to girls being underdiagnosed in childhood, but research suggests it may also be due to ADHD symptoms presenting later in girls than boys. One of the conditions listed in the DSM-5 for an ADHD diagnosis is the presence of "several inattentive or hyperactive-impulsive symptoms ... before age 12 years".[377] However, research is finding that noticeable ADHD symptoms may not emerge for many girls until they are young adults, when the everyday structure of "parents, rules, chores, and daily mandatory school"[375,381-383] changes and they are expected to create their own routines and intrinsic motivators.[375,381-383] Actions that become simple routines for neurotypical adults don't become automatic for neurodivergent people.[375] The challenges with executive function that a person might experience as a result—like with grocery shopping, making meals, or remembering where they put down their phone—can be "embarrassing and exhausting".[375]

Many people know what it feels like to experience guilt or shame if they forget to respond to a text message, neglect the laundry for another weekend, or order takeaway food for the fourth time this week. We are burdened by the perceived expectations of ourselves and others. We discussed earlier how these pressures manifest in relation to our bodies, homes, and gender roles, but they can apply to any of the choices and obstacles we experience, from the mundane to the significant. This negative perception of self can be especially challenging for neurodivergent adults, whose executive dysfunction sometimes actively prevents them from acting in ways they want to. It doesn't matter that we know what we need to do, that it will benefit us in some way, or that it won't take very long; executive dysfunction can be paralysing.[384]

Although executive dysfunction is the most common phrase used to describe this paralysis, another term that I find more accurately aligns with my experience is "inertia".[385] While executive dysfunction describes an inability to perform actions like thinking flexibly, planning ahead, or completing day-to-day tasks, inertia specifically refers to having difficulty with *momentum*—we often know what to do and how to do it, but have trouble switching from one state to another.[384,385] Sometimes inertia can make me lie in bed until 6:59am, despite knowing that my first work call is at 7:00am. That same inertia can make it hard to resist playing the latest videogame I'm obsessed with all weekend because I'd rather do that than anything else, despite knowing it's better for my mental health to fill my weekend with a range of activities, social engagements, and chores. This choice—which never feels quite like a *choice*—can make me feel lazy, rude, and like I'm a failure.

But inertia is also the reason I have been so productive throughout my life, often overachieving to the point of burning myself out. My inability to shift focus can make me so immersed in a task that I forget to eat lunch, or make it difficult to finish work for the day until my current project is complete. It makes it nearly impossible to find balance: I either give something my full attention or I neglect it, both of which have negative ramifications for my well-being. Going for a walk sometimes feels too difficult because I need to check the weather, put on a jacket, leave my apartment, go down the elevator, and exit through the foyer. But once I'm outside, I could happily spend hours walking by the river, watching my dog Biscuit run circles in the grass. Engaging with even the simplest pagan practices, like lighting a candle or doing a five minute grounding exercise, can feel like an impossibility—not because it is difficult, but because it requires me to stop what I am doing and start something else.

Executive dysfunction, or inertia, is a common challenge for neurodivergent adults. However, adults find it more difficult to be diagnosed with ADHD than children, as there's a persistent belief that ADHD is a children's condition that people grow out of as they age. Studies show ADHD continues to impact adults in different ways, can fluctuate over time based on internal and external factors, and symptoms can be flared up by triggers like stress or lack of sleep.[386] There are societal assumptions that boys are more likely to have ADHD than girls and that adults are less likely to experience symptoms.[382] These assumptions, along with the later onset of symptoms in girls than boys, can all lead to women not seeking a diagnosis, being misdiagnosed, or otherwise having trouble finding proper care for the ways their condition impacts their lives.[382]

I was not immune to these biases. Despite having several friends with ADHD and finding similarities between their challenges and my own, I assumed that although they had the condition, I couldn't. After all, I did well when I was at school, I kept my house relatively organised, and I didn't always have trouble concentrating. This certainty was partially due to my lack of understanding about how ADHD presents in adults. I was judging myself based on a stereotype, and not actual research on the condition. When my psychologist tested me for autism, she decided to test me for ADHD as well because she saw some of those traits in me based on our sessions. I agreed, because I decided I might as well see if there was any merit to the comparisons I sometimes drew between myself and my diagnosed friends. I completed the Adult ADHD Self-Report Scale (ASRS) and was taken aback to discover I'd scored more than 99.6% of people in my age and gender bracket for ADHD symptoms. So, factoring in my AQ-50, CAT-Q, and ASRS scores, as well as the experiences and challenges we discussed in our sessions, my psychologist determined that I likely have both ASD and ADHD.

I wonder if I might have received a diagnosis earlier if society had a better understanding of both of these conditions, the way they present in different people, and that they aren't something to be ashamed about? Would my family or I have sought out a diagnosis sooner if we weren't influenced by stereotypes and stigma? And how might that diagnosis have changed my experiences at school or home?

Expanding our understanding of conditions like ASD and ADHD is vital. We need to include all of the different permutations and presentations we are still discovering in our research samples, and expand our studies to include an intersectional range of genders, ages, and backgrounds.

Still, even as we begin to understand that autistic special interests present differently, or that ADHD may have a later onset for girls, it's vital to remember that this too is a generalisation designed simply to show that the diagnostic criteria is currently too narrow. It's important that we don't fall into the trap of gender essentialism— or "neurotrash"[369]—in our desire to categorise the lived experiences of certain groups. Although some research has started to find interesting trends by examining autistic people's brains, genes, and the hormonal make-up of their embryonic fluid, these studies are doing little to account for trans and nonbinary people.[362,363] While biology is fascinating, I am far more interested in the burgeoning field of sociopolitical research that explores how people with ASD struggle with traditional gender norms and, in response, are questioning and challenging them.[362] The way autism and ADHD presents in different people is likely to be influenced by both their biological sex and their gender identity to some degree.[359] Exploring these intersections through additional research has the potential to teach us more about neurodivergence and gender as broader fields of study.[362]

While wondering how an earlier diagnosis may have altered my childhood is an interesting thought experiment, it's actually an impossibility—and not just because time travel doesn't exist. It was only a decade ago, with the publication of the DSM-5, that medical practitioners were permitted to diagnose somebody with *both* ASD and ADHD.[377,387] Prior to this official change, people had been observing traits of ASD in children with ADHD and vice versa for some time. Some practitioners called for the possibility of dual diagnosis to avoid clinicians incorrectly needing to choose one or the other, thus preventing children from receiving proper treatment.[387] Others suggested we should either expand the description and diagnostic criteria of ASD to include inattentive factors or even consider that ASD and ADHD might be different manifestations of the same condition.[388,389] Of those who believe these conditions are distinct but can be comorbid, there is disagreement on the prevalence. Some estimate the number of autistic children that also have ADHD is 13-18%, others state it's 30%, and some consider it as high as 50%, 70%, or even 80%.[388-391] Similarly, estimates for children with ADHD who also present signs of ASD vary from 20-50%, and some listing it as high as 66%.[389,391]

It's clear more research is required to fully understand the relationship between ASD and ADHD. However, regardless of the true percentage, the ability to give people a dual diagnosis unlocks new treatment options. Children with ADHD who struggle socially might benefit from social and speech therapies originally developed to help autistic kids.[387] Similarly, children with autism who have challenges caused by hyperactivity, inattentiveness, or impulsivity may benefit from strategies and treatments designed to help with ADHD.[387] However, it's already difficult for people to receive a diagnosis for either of these conditions, and acknowledging comorbidities introduces a new challenge as it prevents somebody neatly fitting into a diagnostic box.[390] This can make it even more difficult for a clinician to identify a person's condition and can even discourage a person from seeking out a diagnosis. If an individual sees other people with ASD or ADHD and finds it difficult to relate to their experiences, they might talk themselves out of the suspicion they are neurodivergent at all, which is something I often found myself doing before my psychologist suggested we explore it further.

Perhaps an overall diagnosis is less beneficial for suggesting treatments and strategies than understanding the motivations and causes underpinning a person's actions.[528] Social challenges can stem from not being able to process social rules or from impulsive behaviours causing a person to miss social boundaries. Attention issues could be due to a tendency to become distracted or experiencing a level of concentration and hyperfocus that is hard to interrupt.[387] In handling these challenges and teaching a person strategies to overcome them, the approach should change based on the motivations of the individual.

One particular challenge for people with both autism and ADHD—colloquially called auDHD—is that sometimes the traits of one condition can externally appear to cancel out the other, despite the inner turmoil still being severe for the individual.[392] This is something I can relate to. I've always felt like there are contradictions in what I want and need, but have only recently been able to fully understand why. My ASD craves routine but my ADHD struggles to maintain it; my ASD becomes overstimulated while my ADHD is understimulated and I'm paralysed by what to do in response. Or I feel hypocritical because I need my surroundings to be quieter because of my ASD, but then I can't properly filter my own volume because of my ADHD.[390] I've also found different environments and situations tend to bring out different traits, almost like I have a series of dials in my head that get turned up or down in different settings.

I think this is why I did well at school. Where some people with ADHD find sitting still and concentrating for long periods boring, I was able to subconsciously turn up the volume on my ASD and thrive in the routine. I was also naturally quite clever, which helps to mask ADHD; children with above average intellect—"gifted"[383] children—can use that intelligence to compensate for the challenges their ADHD creates for them. This continues until suddenly the complexity of the work exceeds their natural talent. I can distinctly remember the moment this happened to me: I had always received excellent grades in English until my first assignment of year twelve, where I handed in a draft that my teacher told me was not at my usual standard. I completely rewrote that assignment multiple times, until my teacher told me she couldn't review drafts for me anymore. On the final submission, I received a B+. I'd never received a B in English before and I did not know how to process it. I had written it the way I usually did, but for some reason that wasn't good enough anymore. Meanwhile, my teacher thought I hadn't tried hard enough. It impacted my mental health—and this is a pattern in children with ADHD who might receive high grades in school and university while experiencing underlying "chronic anxiety, all-night study sessions, homework that takes way too long to complete, struggles with procrastination, and last-minute completion of papers and projects".[383]

Children who are both gifted and have some sort of developmental or learning difficulty were given the moniker "twice exceptional" or "2e" in the mid-1990s,[393] and I see a lot of myself in the characteristics that are common for this group. Strengths like a broad vocabulary, high creativity, and insights into complex issues are coupled with challenges such as poor social skills, sensitivity to criticism, and stubbornness.[394,395] However, I'm not a fan of the 2e terminology—most days I have a hard time considering myself even *once* exceptional, let alone twice. It's hard to get out of thought patterns I've harboured for years: my tendency towards procrastination is just laziness, my habit of accidentally interrupting others is just rudeness, and my difficulties verbally articulating my feelings is just stupidity. When you are intelligent in some areas, your challenges are met with "but you're smart, you should be better than this" and you internalise that as "I'm a failure". It is a shared experience that other neurodivergent people have expressed too.[375]

This is how it felt at school sometimes. I received good grades, but I struggled to make friends and I often misunderstood social dynamics or became the target of bullying. I generally assumed this was just because I was "a nerd" but there were other intelligent people in my grade who understood jokes or knew the difference between "appropriate" and "too far". I remember once in preschool, another child and I were sent outside to bring in the wooden prams we had all been playing with earlier. My peer decided to bring in the pram I liked more, and I bit him so he'd give it to me, without fully realising the extremity of my actions. Not exactly reasonable social behaviour. (Sorry, Jayden.)

Since being diagnosed, I've spent a lot of time doing this: digging back through memories of my childhood and finding signs that, in hindsight, make it clear my brain processes the world in a way that is different from most of the people around me. My *fussiness* with food can be attributed to food selectivity common in autistic people; the facial tics and hand-washing compulsions I had in school were also possibly a symptoms of ASD and a response to overstimulation; and the fact that executive function is easy for me some days and impossible on others is not a personal failing but an indicator of ADHD. Understanding these challenges, being able to attribute them to neurodivergence, and finally learning coping strategies tailored to how my brain processes the world has been revolutionary—and this experience is also mirrored by others who receive a diagnosis as an adult.[293] Understanding our diagnoses also helps us articulate our challenges to others, improve our self-esteem by helping us understand behaviours and experiences that previously felt like personal failings, and can reduce feelings of isolation and anxiety.[396]

Anxiety is something I've always struggled with. I went to a doctor and was diagnosed with generalised anxiety disorder and depression when I was a teenager, and when I described the moments where I became so overwhelmed it was debilitating, I was told I'd been having panic attacks. I'd never questioned that until recently, when I realised it's more likely I have been experiencing autistic meltdowns or shutdowns for most of my life. While both of these reactions can involve feeling anxious, overwhelmed, and overstimulated, I don't experience the racing heart rate and the fear that I'm dying that are hallmarks of a panic attack.[397] Instead, during my worst episodes, I have an unmanageable build-up of energy and lose control over my actions and thoughts. I spiral into self-hatred and guilt, I hit myself, I struggle to make eye contact, and I am unable to comprehend what is going on around me. These are extremely common signs of autistic meltdowns or shutdowns.[398] It's a wildly frustrating experience because I feel like my rational and reasonable self is still in my brain, but has been locked away from the controls.

More than a decade ago, my doctor didn't know any better, and he sent me to see a psychologist for my panic attacks. It was not my first time seeing a therapist of some kind—I'd been seeing counsellors since I was twelve due to spiralling thoughts and depressive tendencies, but none had been particularly impactful. I thought this might be different though: I now had an official diagnosis of a mental health condition and I was seeing somebody outside the school or university system. I don't remember the psychologist's name, but I do remember the only advice she gave me during that session: you are the sky and your depression is the clouds. The analogy was designed to teach me that depression is temporary and I am constant, but I knew that already. I didn't want metaphors; I wanted solutions.

I avoided therapy for a while after that, but I continued to struggle. I tried again in my early 20s, but received little insight. I tried again a few years later, and met a therapist who I actually enjoyed seeing, but he moved interstate before I could make much progress. I tried another therapist, but three sessions in he interrupted the session to ask whether or not I *liked* him. I revisited therapy *again* in my late-20s, and this time was very successful, but it was specifically for couples counselling and I couldn't see the same psychologist for myself. Finally, after eight attempts, I found the psychologist who ended up helping me discover my neurodivergence, and she helped me find strategies and answers that have started to improve my quality of life.

About halfway through my psychologist search—and halfway through my 20s—I seriously considered medication for my mental health for the first time. I had always avoided it because I was scared that I would lose part of myself if I numbed my anxiety. Sometimes it felt like the only thing driving me to get out of bed and achieve anything with my life was the panic about what would happen if I didn't. With the help of a new doctor, I tried a couple of SSRIs until I found one that actually helped. It had a huge impact on my general sense of happiness and wellbeing. I could sleep through the night without being woken by night terrors, I could break myself out of the thought spirals I sometimes found myself in, and I found myself getting excited about things again. I still felt like myself, just *better*.

I'm still on SSRIs now. I occasionally take a break from them to see how my brain is doing without pharmaceutical intervention, but I'm met with the return of nightmares, panic spirals, and overstimulated shutdowns. My brain seems to benefit from the extra serotonin it has at its disposal when my SSRI blocks my nerve cells from reabsorbing it.[399] Serotonin is responsible for "modulat[ing] neural activity and a wide range of neuropsychological processes"[399] such as mood regulation, with research finding it has an impact on a range of other biological systems such as the heart, bowels, bladder, and reproductive system.

Serotonin is so versatile because it's a neurohormone, meaning it can enter the circulatory system like a hormone but can also bind to receptors in the brain like a neurotransmitter—

and depending also on its form, it can have different impacts on our bodies.[400,401] Because of its many uses and beneficial effects, it's the source of ongoing research, which can sometimes be misconstrued or misunderstood. For example, wellbeing blogs have learned that tryptophan is a precursor to serotonin and are therefore insisting people should eat more foods with high tryptophan content, like eggs, cheese, and tofu, as it will improve their mood.[402] While it is true that the brain can turn tryptophan into serotonin, for this to work, the body needs to move this amino acid to the central nervous system.[403] Amino acids compete for transport with several other essential amino acids, meaning very little of it actually reaches the brain through this avenue and eating more omelettes is unlikely to make a noticeable difference to your mood (unless you *really* like omelettes).

Serotonin is not the only "feel good"[400] chemical subject to rumours being shared through the wellness industry. It's one of four neurohormones that impact our mood and other biological systems: serotonin, endorphins, dopamine, and oxytocin.[400,401] With the wellbeing industry seeking quick fixes to improve our moods, all of these chemicals are currently under scrutiny and are the target of misinformation.[404]

For example, when researching endorphins, I found a chiropractor who claims that adrenaline is what causes endorphins to be released, while a law firm's blog post describes adrenaline as a type of endorphin.[405,406] These were two of the highest search results on the topic, and they're not true. While stress can cause both adrenaline and endorphins to be released, adrenaline is one of three catecholamine hormones released from the adrenal gland above the kidneys, while endorphins are peptide hormones released from the pituitary gland in the brain.[407] They work together to support our body when we need increased strength, reflexes, and pain resistance, but they are—as far as we currently understand—separate systems.[408,409]

The law firm's blog makes another claim that sounds sensationalist when it compares endorphins to opiates, however, this is actually true.[406,410] When they are acting as neurotransmitters, endorphins bind to the same receptors in our brains as opiate medications and can help relieve pain and stress.[411]

Dopamine makes us feel good in another way: this neurohormone is released when we achieve something and is designed to reward us for beneficial behaviours.[412] When it occurs in our brains, dopamine can reinforce actions that make us feel happy and productive. It's the chemical that makes ticking an item off our to-do lists feel so good. But dopamine can also be released when we engage in unhealthy habits, and reinforce negative cycles. It's such an effective motivator that it can lead to addictive behaviours, especially with substances like nicotine, alcohol, and other drugs that activate the dopamine receptors in our brain.[413]

Oxytocin is associated with relationships, affection, and physical touch.[414] Humans are social creatures and, as a neurotransmitter, oxytocin is designed to make us feel good when we bond with others to help encourage us to develop relationships and trust, and to alleviate loneliness and stress.[414] The giddy feeling at the beginning of a relationship is due to an increased level of oxytocin, and it's the same chemical that makes us happy when we spend time with a pet.[415,416] When oxytocin operates in the bloodstream, it's associated with reproductive processes; it's released during sex, and is the hormone that induces labour and initiates lactation in breast-feeding parents.[414]

Dopamine, oxytocin, serotonin, and endorphins (DOSE) can all help us feel happy and relaxed in different ways. It makes sense that, upon learning this, the wellbeing industry started pursuing ways to increase these neurohormones in our brains and bloodstreams. But unfortunately there's no quick fix for our emotional state, and it takes more than eating cheese or even taking an SSRI to improve our mental health. It takes repeatedly doing things that make us happy to create the required neural pathways for that to influence our day-to-day life. It's similar to going to the gym. One session is not going to make you strong; you need to go back multiple times over a long duration to see the positive impact.

The gym is not just a convenient analogy— it's also a proven way of boosting DOSE levels and therefore possibly happiness and relaxation over time.[417] Exercise releases endorphins, and can boost serotonin and dopamine levels.[417] Laughter also produces dopamine, and so can getting a good night's sleep.[418,419] Our oxytocin levels can be increased with hugs and kisses, and spending time with people and animals whom we love.[416,420] Sunlight can help us produce serotonin, as can practices like mindfulness or gratitude journaling.[421,422] Music releases dopamine and serotonin, meditation increases dopamine and endorphin production, and massages can trigger serotonin, dopamine, and endorphins.[416,423-427]

But it's important to remember not everything that boosts our feel good chemicals is inherently good, and long term strategies for improving mental health are more complicated than putting on some music or laughing at a good joke. Mental illness is an incredibly common comorbidity with neurodivergence, especially when the latter remains undiagnosed—and no amount of exercise or gratitude journaling can make up for the low self-esteem, isolation, and frustration that drives these mental health outcomes.[428,429] Girls are particularly susceptible to the mental health risks of neurodivergence, possibly because they are less likely to be diagnosed. Spending more time unable to properly function in a neurotypical society, feeling isolated from peers, and perceiving yourself as a failure can lead to anxiety, depression, self-harm, and suicidal ideation.[361,430] I am relatively lucky in that my anxiety and depression were identified early, but despite that, they were poorly handled by school counsellors and weren't diagnosed until my late teens. I self-harmed in high school, not because I wanted to hurt myself, but because I enjoyed watching my wounds heal. I didn't understand my brain sometimes and why I was hurting internally, but cuts on my fingers would always reliably stitch back together in a way that helped me feel like maybe I could heal internally too.

I'm still working on it. I understand my brain more now than I used to, and I'm learning strategies to deal with my mental health conditions and neurodivergence in equal measure. The distinction between mental health and neurodivergence is blurry: perhaps the difference is that we develop one and are born with the other, that one is entirely negative while the other provides some positive traits, or that we strive to cure one while we learn to live with the other.[431,432] But the lines in my brain between my ASD, my anxiety, my ADHD, my depression, and even my fibromyalgia are messy and undefined. The person I am is influenced by all of them; they all bring me benefits and challenges in equal (or maybe not *equal*) measure, and I'm learning to be okay with them all.

BOTANY, MEDICINE, AND REDISCOVERING NATURE

When I was a child, I used to collect all sorts of things. I'd brew potions made from mud and lilly pilly berries, I'd sort feathers into little bags based on colour and size, and I'd press flowers in the pages of books. It was sometimes difficult to stop me from picking up every shiny black rock that had detached itself from the asphalt and was discarded on the side of the road.

People have always brought the outdoors in. Unlike tarot cards, flower arranging actually *does* date back to ancient Egypt, where, as early as 2,500 BCE, people were putting flowers in vases and garlands, and bringing them into their homes and tombs.[433] Following Christian conversion, pagan Europeans would place evergreens in their living spaces at New Year to scare away the Devil— many people in Western societies still do similar, as part of our Christmas celebrations.[434] Flowers were given as gifts in Victorian England, with each type of flower chosen to convey coded meanings (which were outlined in the "flower dictionaries"[433] that became increasingly popular at the time).[435] It's still common today to give flowers to loved ones to mark milestones, show affection, or ask forgiveness.

The Western world seems to have become especially preoccupied with bringing plants inside during the 21st century. Homeware stores like IKEA are overflowing with houseplants, encouraging us to "blur the lines between inside and out with plants",[436] and "have a sense of nature invited right into your home".[436] The environment is a common topic of conversation right now as we navigate the unpredictable weather and natural disasters that accompany climate change, and perhaps our obsession with houseplants is one way we're making sense of that overwhelming catastrophe. We are grieving for a natural world we will never be able to return to by turning it into furnishings—rattan dressers, floral wallpaper, and *houseplants*. It's akin to how "futurism"[437] became trendy decor in the 1950s and 60s, when pod-shaped furniture, rocket-inspired lamps, and the latest gadgetry helped Americans contextualise technological questions about the space race and atomic warfare.[437]

Buying bouquets of flowers and indoor plants is the most obvious way that we—in the words of IKEA—invite a sense of nature into our homes. However, it's also in the vial of lavender oil you use to help you sleep, the coffee beans and teabags in your pantry, and the capsules you keep in your medicine cabinet. But, even though we spend every day surrounded by nature—whether we know it or not—most people aren't really paying attention. The only individuals who *really* look at the leaves on the trees we pass by seem to be botanists, children who are trying to make a magic potion out of mud and lilly pilly berries, and my grandfather.

When I was younger and my grandparents came to visit, my family would go for walks. On every walk, we would discover partway through our journey that my grandfather, Kev, was no longer with the group. He would inevitably be several paces behind, staring at a leaf. He could determine the species of a tree or diagnose a plant's illness just by looking at its leaves. Occasionally he'd crush a leaf and hand it to me to smell; whenever I smell lemon myrtle, I'm transported back to his garden.

When Kev stopped to identify a tree from its leaves, he was performing phytomorphology. Phytomorphology is focused on the external appearance and visual identification of plants, rather than other branches of botanical science that are dedicated to the internal and microscopic study of plant anatomy.[438] Some of the terms used by phytomorphologists most of us would recognise (e.g. roots, trunk, branches, leaves, fruit). Although these terms give us a general understanding of a tree's architecture, they are too vague to help us distinguish one tree species from another.

For example, I want you to imagine a leaf. What colour is it? What shape? Are the edges smooth, or do they have ridges or notches? What patterns do the veins make along the leaf's surface?

The leaf you are picturing could be vastly different to the one I am imagining, but both of them are still recognisably *leaves*. Leaves might be broad and flat to absorb more sunlight or curved to catch water. They could be grouped in fronds like a palm or fern, or tightly rolled into a cylinder like a pine needle. Leaves can be classified as having more than fifty different shapes—elliptical, oval, truncate, lanceolate, or linear.[439,440] They might have smooth edges or ridges, teeth, and indentations. Smooth edges (like on a beech tree) are referred to as an entire margin, while teeth might be dentate or serrate, depending on whether they're pointing forwards (like most poplar leaves) or outwards (like a strawberry leaf). Leaves with larger curved indentations (like an oak) have lobed margins, and the spaces between the lobes are called sinuses.

Examining a leaf even closer, you can see the veins on its surface. The different patterns these veins make is called "venation"[439]–the same term used to describe the system of blood vessels in an animal. When a leaf extends from a tree, it often attaches to the stem with a thick vein called a petiole, which allows the leaf to rotate to face the Sun (although some leaves connect to the plant's stem directly and these are called sessile leaves). Sometimes veins extend from a single point—the top of the petiole—and fan outwards. This pattern occurs on palmate leaves. Pinnate leaves have just one vein that extends straight up from the petiole (called the midrib) and smaller veins branch out from it as if it is, itself, the trunk of a tiny tree.

Just as our veins move nutrients and oxygen through our body, veins transport nutrients and fluids through a tree from its roots through to its leaves.[441] Although, instead of using blood, trees have sap flowing through their branches, stems, and petioles. All plants have sap, although some varieties are more visible to the human eye than others. Sap can sometimes have a sweet taste and be used as a sugar substitute or syrup. The most common example of this is maple tree sap (which is used to make maple syrup).[442] Sap can also be used to make wound dressings and soaps. For example, sap from the Australian blushwood tree has antimicrobial properties and can help clean lacerations.[443]

In addition to sap, some plants also produce liquids like latexes and resins. While sap works inside the plant to carry nutrients, both resin and latex work outside the plant. Resin—sometimes referred to as pitch or tar—is usually produced if the plant is cut or injured. It works to naturally seal a plant's injury, closing the wound so it can heal while also keeping bugs and other pests out.[444] Resin tends to be thicker and stickier than sap, and has traditionally been used as a waterproofing aid, especially in shipbuilding. Some resins can also be distilled into essential oils (like frankincense or myrrh), or can be dried into gemstones (like amber).[445] Latex serves a similar purpose to resin but has a different chemical makeup, causing it to be thinner than resin and have a "milky" appearance.[446] Both resin and latex are initially liquids (although their viscosity differs) and coagulate on exposure to air.

Colloquially, we use the word latex to refer to the specific latex that comes from the rubber tree, *Hevea brasiliensis,* which we use to make everything from medical gloves to car tires.[589] However, varieties of latex are produced by approximately 10% of flowering plant species, and some of these are useful for other reasons.[448] For example, *Papaver somniferum* (the opium poppy or breadseed poppy) produces a latex from which we derive opium and other analgesics.[449]

Latexes contain many different compounds, including alkaloids, proteins, starches, sugars, oils, and tannins. In the opium poppy, the alkaloids are the element used for its medicinal properties. Alkaloids are naturally occurring compounds containing at least one nitrogen atom. Many alkaloids have pronounced physiological effects on humans, and can be used as medical treatments, psychotropic drugs, or poisons. The six alkaloids that naturally occur in the largest quantities in the latex of the opium poppy are morphine, narcotine, codeine, thebaine, papaverine, and narceine. Of these, morphine, codeine, and thebaine have analgesic properties and are internationally controlled substances. These are referred to as opiates. Opiates impact humans by targeting the opioid receptors in the central nervous system— the same ones used by endorphins to regulate a person's pain and temperature, as well as controlling sensory perceptions.[67]

Morphine was first isolated from opium poppy latex in 1804 by pharmacist and chemist Friedrich Sertürner, and this is generally believed to be the first isolation of an active ingredient from a plant.[450] Since that discovery, poppies have been manipulated through selective breeding to increase their analgesic alkaloid content.[450] Morphine and codeine are still used as medicines today, while thebaine is used to synthesise other common analgesics like oxycodone, hydrocodone, and hydromorphone.[450] Heroin (diamorphine) is also derived from morphine, although it is combined with other synthetic components to make the drug up to three times more potent than its source.[450] These semi-synthetic drugs derived from opium are known as opioids, although some sources have begun to use the terms opiate (naturally occurring) and opioid (partially or completely synthetic) interchangeably.

Although the alkaloids in opium poppy latex were only identified and isolated in the last couple of centuries, the latex itself has been harvested and used for medicinal purposes since before people kept written records. Although some cultural artefacts suggest it may have been earlier, it is generally agreed that opiates were first used as analgesics in approximately 3400 BCE in lower Mesopotamia.[451] (Mesopotamia was located in West Asia, and occupied the area that is now Iraq, as well as parts of Iran, Turkey, Syria, and Kuwait.) Opium has been used by people for longer than any other substance—including alcohol—and has had significant impacts on human history.[450] Before we developed ways to synthesise alkaloids, opium poppy latex was harvested by scoring the fruit of the opium poppy, causing the latex to leak out as it tried to heal the plant's injuries. When the latex dried on the surface of the fruit, it was scraped off and dehydrated before use. This substance was referred to as *opion* by the ancient Greeks, which is where it derived its contemporary name opium.

Opiates are not the only alkaloids that humans use to manipulate our physiology. Caffeine is an alkaloid many people use everyday to wake up in the morning.[452] Other addictive substances like nicotine and cocaine are also alkaloids.[453,454]

Although people have been using plants to treat illnesses and ailments for millennia, analysing the chemical composition of plants and isolating compounds like alkaloids has allowed us to better determine *why* certain plants have specific effects on people. The study of the chemical compounds found in plants is called phytochemistry. Phytochemistry isn't restricted to discussions at universities and research conferences. In fact, we've already discussed many findings from this field within this book. As well as influencing medicine, phytochemistry informs a lot of nutritional science by examining plant-based carbohydrates, proteins, and fats, as well as vitamins and minerals.

Sugars—also known as saccharides—are the most common form of carbohydrate occurring in nature. There are four types of saccharide: monosaccharides, disaccharides, oligosaccharides, and polysaccharides. Although these terms don't come up often in our day-to-day lives, some specific types of sugars have more recognisable names. Glucose (found in vegetables and honey) and fructose (found in fruit) are both examples of monosaccharides, while lactose (found in dairy products) and sucrose (found in white sugar) are disaccharides. Starch and dietary fibre are also types of sugar, specifically polysaccharides.

The main difference between these four types of sugar is simply the number of monosaccharide groups they contain: disaccharides have two groups connected to each other, oligosaccharides generally have between three and twelve, and polysaccharides generally have greater than twelve.

This is why monosaccharides are called simple sugars, disaccharides are complex sugars, and the other groups generally aren't referred to as sugars at all (despite our bodies turning them back into simple sugars during digestion). The simpler the saccharide is when we consume it, the easier—and quicker—it is for us to digest. That's why if you eat something with simple sugars (like a piece of fruit or a handful of lollies) you receive energy in one quick burst rather than over a prolonged period, whereas the energy is released more slowly if you eat something containing more complex carbohydrates (like bread or rice).[455]

Understanding the science behind sugar isn't just interesting; I've found it has completely changed the way I think about the food I eat. Society—specifically the diet industry—has tried to convince us certain foods are *good* or *bad*, but the chemical difference between the foods at the top and bottom of the controversial food pyramid aren't as significant as we have been made to believe.[456,457,193] More importantly, there's certainly no inherent moral value that can be applied to the number of saccharides a particular item of food contains. Sometimes a situation calls for a simple sugar, like eating a bar of chocolate before a race or an exam.

Our bodies produce many specific enzymes dedicated to breaking down different complex sugars into their monosaccharides.[458] Generally, this process happens without us giving it much thought, but if you're missing some of the enzymes you need, it can result in abdominal pain and gastrointestinal issues. Lactose intolerance is a particularly well-known example of this, and is caused when the body doesn't create enough of an enzyme called lactase. Our bodies need lactase to break lactose down into its monosaccharides: glucose and galactose. Over-the-counter medications designed to help with lactose intolerance simply introduce more of this enzyme into our digestive system.[459]

Irritable bowel syndrome (IBS) is another gastrointestinal condition that may be helped by introducing additional enzymes into the digestive system.[460] IBS can be a standalone condition, or a symptom of other illnesses, like fibromyalgia.[461] IBS can be caused by a range of factors, such as the speed that food moves through the intestines, hypersensitive nerves, and stress. Some research is suggesting that IBS could also be caused by the body producing an inadequate number of certain enzymes, similar to what happens with lactose intolerance.[460] This aligns with my own experience of the condition; my IBS tends to flare-up because of how *much* of a particular food group I've eaten, rather than the foods themselves, possibly because my body hasn't been able to produce enough enzymes to counter what I've consumed. It's only a theory at this stage, but the study of phytochemistry is helping us learn about our bodies and may hold answers for people who experience acute and chronic pain as a result of consuming certain foods.

In addition to their use in food, saccharides have other medical uses. For example, polysaccharides tend to have a jelly-like consistency and have traditionally been applied to skin irritations (e.g. the substance found within the leaves of aloe vera).[462] Some sugars also bond with other compounds to create glycosides, many of which have medical and other uses.[463] There are many types of glycoside, depending on the compound that the sugar has attached to. For example, cardiac glycosides are used in the treatment of heart diseases; flavonoids can have anti-inflammatory effects; saponins produce a soap-like lather and have antibacterial qualities; and cyanogenic glycosides can be used as muscle relaxants in small doses.

Another area of phytochemistry that nutritional science has become preoccupied with is the identification of vitamins and minerals in plants. I've already mentioned a few times that we first identified vitamins in the early 1900s when, using phytochemistry, we discovered that there are several substances necessary for our health that we are unable to make ourselves—we need to *consume* them.[187] There are 13 vitamins that humans cannot synthesise, which are called "essential vitamins".[464] They include vitamins A, C, D, E, and K, as well as several varieties of B vitamins. All of these can be found in plants except two; vitamin B12 is predominantly found in animal products (but can also be found in some fungi and seaweed), and vitamin D is synthesised through exposure to sunlight.[465,466]

Because we are reliant on consuming these substances to remain healthy, it's possible for us to have vitamin or mineral deficiencies. Some common examples include scurvy (lack of vitamin C), beriberi (lack of vitamin B1), rickets (lack of vitamin D), and iron-deficiency anaemia.[187] When it was first discovered that these deficiencies can lead to illnesses, there was a period where some scientists believed *all* diseases could be cured if we found the right vitamin. This prompted several decades of the nutrition and medical fields exploring the health benefits of each of these substances.

This preoccupation with improving nutrition as a way to treat illnesses and diseases led to the formation of naturopathy, an alternative medicine practice based on the health benefits of herbal remedies and lifestyle changes, including diet, exercise, sleep, and stress reduction.[467] Although naturopathy as a form of medical education was only established in the early 1900s, naturopaths consider their practice to have started with Hippocrates, who prescribed changes to diet and exercise to treat diseases such as diabetes during the fourth century BCE.[468,469]

Hippocrates made many contributions to modern medicine, including creating terminology like acute and chronic conditions, introducing the concept of using tubes (or pipes) to drain fluid from abscesses, and performing the first recorded endoscopy.[470-472] But don't forget Hippocrates was also responsible for concepts like the wandering womb. I remind you of this to make a simple point: just because Hippocrates said it was true, doesn't necessarily mean it's scientifically proven.

Regardless, Hippocrates was trying his best to help people who were suffering from a range of medical conditions we didn't yet understand. He contemplated whether our bodies became ill when our "humours"[473] were unbalanced, and suggested methods for adjusting our levels of black bile, yellow bile, blood, and phlegm. He also posited that miasma may be the cause of our diseases, and suggested ways to reduce the "foul air"[473] that passed between individuals and caused us to get sick. Humours and miasma remained part of medical discourse until the mid-1800s, when germ theory and the identification of viruses redirected medical research.[70]

When viruses were discovered in the 1890s, there was a boom in bacteriology.[474] This, in turn, led to more rigorous scientific methods being applied when reproducing results and recommending treatments. In the mid-1900s, medical training in the Western world shifted from a mix of institutions and practices with varying levels of efficacy, to a model that resembles what we mean when we say "modern medicine" today.[475] In the United Kingdom, this was marked by the publication of the 1944 Report of the Inter-Departmental Committee on Medical Schools.[476] This report listed a number of recommendations for medical schools, including, most notably, guidelines for the clinical facilities medical schools needed to have, and the provision that newly qualified doctors must complete a period of hospital-based training before being able to practise independently.[477] The report also mandated that schools would not receive payments unless they admitted a "reasonable proportion" of female students.[477]

In part, I mention this report because the UK's medical school system has always influenced Australia's, which is relevant to the medical care I've been receiving my entire life. (I also mention this report because the Inter-Departmental Committee on Medical Schools was chaired by a man called Sir William Goodenough, and this means the report is sometimes called the *Goodenough Report*, and that made me smile and felt worth sharing.)[478]

We've made remarkable scientific progress in recent years. We first saw an atom under a microscope in 1955.[479] We first walked on the Moon in 1969.[480] The first iPhone went on sale in 2007.[481] We are so used to our day-to-day life we forget just how *new* this normal is. Having doctors who wash their hands is revolutionary, let alone having reliable medical treatment for a range of conditions and diseases.[482]

Our newfound faith in scientific discoveries has led to an immediate distrust of old remedies. In some cases, this is entirely justified—my assertive nature is not due to a wandering uterus and I don't need my vagina fumigated, but thank you for the offer, Hippocrates. However, our scientific progress can also lead to us judging or dismissing the natural treatments that led to our medicinal discoveries in the first place. Just as naturopathy can be guilty of dismissing all conventional medicine as dangerous, allopathic physicians can be too quick to dismiss all herbal remedies as useless.

It's also worth noting that many herbal remedies have been used for centuries by Indigenous populations, who pass their knowledge down through oral tradition. Dismissing herbal remedies in favour of *modern medicine* is a colonial idea designed to make us value some forms of knowledge and record-keeping over others.

Modern medicine is undoubtedly remarkable: infant mortality rates are the lowest they have ever been, smallpox has been eradicated, and we developed multiple effective vaccines for the COVID-19 pandemic within a year of the virus being identified.[483-485] But traditional remedies are amazing too: communities in South America have been using the bark of the *Cinchona calisaya* tree to treat malaria since before we knew what malaria *was*, and quinine—the alkaloid found in the bark—is still used in the treatment of malaria today.[486] The assumptions that Western society has made (and continues to make) about the medicinal knowledge of Indigenous peoples and the impact colonialism has had on Indigenous populations is causing Indigenous languages to die out, along with their knowledge of medicinal plants.[487]

The formalisation of the scientific method has led to significant improvements in medical science. However, it is also important to recognise that evidence-based medicine is not as objective and unbiased as some allopathic physicians want us to believe. For a particular condition or treatment to receive the multiple peer-reviewed studies it requires to be considered scientifically proven or understood, scientists with the relevant skills and organisations with the necessary funding both need to take an interest in that topic.[488] That means some conditions receive a lot more attention than others.[488]

Even when issues are given scientific attention, the research methods used can exclude certain individuals or groups. For example, in some medical studies, men are the majority (or all) of the participants in their clinical trials, meaning there is limited, or no, research on how particular conditions or medications differently impact women and other genders.[488] This is evident when comparing research into fibromyalgia to other ailments. Fibromyalgia can be debilitating but research into the condition is relatively recent and incomplete. It means that treatment options for fibromyalgia are still limited and understanding of the condition is lacking, even within the medical field. This can have significant impacts on people with fibromyalgia seeking healthcare or financial support. I'm incredibly lucky my fibromyalgia does not prevent me from working most days and my workplace is understanding and flexible, as people with fibromyalgia are not eligible for payments under the National Disability Insurance Scheme (NDIS) in Australia.[489]

Some preliminary research has been exploring the impacts of caffeine on fibromyalgia pain. Caffeine is an alkaloid found in the leaves, beans, and seeds of plants, including *Coffea* (coffee beans), *Camellia sinensis* (tea leaves), *Theobroma cacao* (cocoa beans), *Cola acuminata* (kola nuts), and *Paullinia cupana* (guarana seeds).[490] People have been making medicinal and everyday products from caffeine for millennia. According to Chinese legend, Shennong first made caffeinated beverages from tea leaves submerged in boiling water as early as 3000 BCE.[68] Kola nuts have been chewed in west Africa to increase energy for centuries, and cacao pod residue was once found inside an ancient Mayan pot. Today, many people consume caffeinated beverages to increase energy, but it is also used to treat pain for some conditions, including migraines.[490]

A recent study found caffeine intake can reduce pain for fibromyalgia sufferers if they are also using opioid medication, but has no impact if they are not on any pain relief.[491] Another study has found caffeine intake can actually have a negative impact on pain levels, especially when consumed daily or in high quantities.[492] Interestingly, neither of these studies reflect my own lived experience. I find caffeine can help with my pain, and I'm not taking any other pain relief medications currently. I don't say this to suggest that the entire medical industry should shift their perspectives based on my own experiences, but rather to remind us that bodies are individual and complicated, and the findings of a population-level study don't apply to every person.

With this in mind, it makes sense that some people rebel against the offerings of conventional medicine. Allopathic medications don't always work, and even when they do, they can come with side effects and other challenges. They can be prescribed to us by physicians who don't fully understand our conditions or who don't believe our symptoms. And they can have scary names.

There is a psychological bias called processing fallacy that can lead to us favouring substances with names that feel familiar over names that are difficult to pronounce or that have "harsh-sounding"[493] syllables. This fallacy leads to proponents of alternative medicine and the wellbeing industry perpetuating chemophobia.[494] Chemophobia presents itself as the belief that chemicals are unnatural, artificial, and harmful substances—rather than recognising chemicals are *all* substances—and is usually caused by a lack of scientific literacy.[494]

The processing fallacy is exemplified by the dihydrogen monoxide parody. This parody has appeared multiple times in newspapers and on websites since the 1980s, with journalists or clever schoolkids warning the population about the use of dihydrogen monoxide.[495] Dihydrogen monoxide is a chemical substance that is a major component of acid rain, can cause severe burns, and accelerates the corrosion of metals. With its unfamiliar name and potential effects, this chemical sounds scary; however, dihydrogen monoxide is simply a chemical name for water. This parody was originally designed to demonstrate how a lack of scientific literacy can lead to misplaced fears directed towards substances that might be innocuous or even essential to our health.[495]

Humans tend to be anxious about anything we don't understand, and the wellbeing industry can perpetuate these fears, suggesting that isolating compounds like alkaloids, saccharides, and other phytochemicals somehow makes them less natural—and, as a result, they are more harmful. Firstly, this neglects to recognise that some substances most toxic to humans are entirely natural, such as mercury, snake venom, and arsenic.[496] Secondly, it falsely suggests that a substance is unnatural simply because it has been separated from other components of its original source, which is like saying a leaf is unnatural simply because it has been removed from the rest of its tree.

I imagine this misplaced concern about isolating compounds comes from preliminary studies that have shown how some compounds have more effective physiological influences on humans when they aren't administered separately, but rather alongside other compounds from their original plant.[497] This is exemplified by the cannabis plant. Cannabis contains many phytochemicals, like all plants, but the two that are most discussed are tetrahydrocannabinol (THC) and cannabidiol (CBD). THC is the compound that gives people a high, while CBD has demonstrated medical benefits for many conditions with zero psychoactive effects. Interestingly, it has been found that CBD is more effective at treating symptoms when used in conjunction with THC and other compounds found in cannabis than by itself.[497] Together these phytochemicals have a synergy that is referred to as an "entourage effect".[497] Basically, they are greater than the sum of their parts.

But it is foolish to take this finding and extend it so that it applies to all plants and their various compounds. In fact, this is another type of informal fallacy, known as a "faulty generalisation".[498] Faulty generalisations occur when you take a small sample and then make incorrect assumptions about what this means for the whole. For example, if you found that some illnesses were caused by vitamin deficiencies, and therefore determined *all* illnesses were caused by this; or if you decided Hippocrates was right about some things, and therefore he was right about *all* things (or, inversely, that he was wrong about some things, and so all of his work should be void).

Generally, compounds have not been found more effective when taken alongside other parts of their source plant—although medical science is always evolving and this could change. However, we should not start assuming this is the case and that science will figure it out some day; in some circumstances, it could cause significantly more harm to humans if we didn't isolate the compounds we used medicinally. For example, *Atropa belladonna* (deadly nightshade) contains an alkaloid called atropine that can be used to dilate pupils, to remedy some forms of poison, and as a topical treatment for conditions like gout.[499] But this plant is called deadly for a reason; in addition to atropine, *Atropa belladonna* contains other alkaloids such as hyoscyamine and scopolamine that are highly toxic to humans. Preparing plants in specific ways allows us to access their helpful compounds and reduce their harmful ones, and various preparation techniques have been used for millennia. The only difference is that now—in addition to traditional processes like soaking, boiling, and macerating—we also use various methods of chemical extraction, which allows us to access new compounds, or isolate existing ones more efficiently.

Before being used for medicinal purposes, leaves, flowers, bark, and other plant material might be cut into smaller pieces, ground into a fine powder, or extracted by soaking or steaming. The resulting compounds can then be consumed whole; added to smoothies, juices, and meals; put inside capsules to easily swallow; or combined with water, oil, or alcohol for any number of applications. The resulting substances all have different names, like extracts, essences, essential oils, and fragrance oils. These can be marketed as similar products, but there are some key variations between them.

The primary difference between extracts and essential oils is the preparation method. While extracts use a liquid to release the medicinal components of a plant, essential oils are created using steam distillation so they are less diluted and more challenging to prepare. While both extracts and essential oils are made from natural products, essences and fragrance oils are synthetic. For example, vanilla extract or essence is commonly used in baking, and while both will smell and taste of vanilla, only an extract is likely to contain natural vanillin. Some essential oils have antiseptic properties, some can assist with pain management, and others have aromas that have been connected with calming psychological impacts.

Extract is a catch-all term used to describe all sorts of products (e.g. infusions, decoctions, ointments, and tinctures). The main difference between each of these is whether they use water, oil, or alcohol to carry the plant material. Both infusions and decoctions use hot water to extract compounds from plant matter. Infusions are typically made from leaves and flowers, which require less time in hot water for their compounds to be extracted. You can make infusions by steeping plant matter in water that has already been heated. Infusions are sometimes also referred to as teas, although technically tea is a specific type of infusion that can only be made from the leaves of the *Camellia sinensis* tea plant.[68] The final product is strained and the liquid is consumed.

Decoctions tend to be made from other parts of a plant, like bark, roots, or dried fruits. Rather than pouring pre-heated water over the plant material as in an infusion, decoctions are made by simmering the plant material in water over a low heat for a prolonged period, allowing the plant matter more time to release its medicinal components. The liquid will evaporate while brewing a decoction, creating a concentrated final product. Broths are a form of decoction, where bones, meat, or vegetables are simmered in water for a prolonged period and then strained to leave a clear liquid with concentrated flavour. Decoctions can be turned into syrups to thicken and preserve them, which are created by combining a decoction with either honey or sugar, or sometimes alcohol.

In instances where an infusion or decoction is specifically designed to promote general health and wellbeing, it can be referred to as a tonic. Tonic herbs are specific herbs that have properties that can help stimulate specific systems and organs. Whether a mixture is a tonic is less to do with how it is prepared or its consistency; rather, it's about its purpose and the plants used to create it.

Poultices (also called a cataplasm) are also made by adding plant material to water; however, this preparation differs both in consistency and application. Poultices are not strained after being prepared, so they have a paste-like consistency. They have traditionally been made by chewing plant material to combine it with saliva, and using the masticated material. Poultices are put directly onto the skin or a wound, rather than ingested, and can be applied either on their own or via a cloth compress. Topical treatments are referred to as liniments or embrocations. The first time I used a poultice was in Sussex, where a herbalist encouraged me to touch a patch of stinging nettles, and then chew a handful of yellow dock to apply to the area. It was interesting to observe that these two plants—one that stings, and one that neutralises—often naturally grow side by side.

Ointments are a common form of liniment that suspend plant products in oil. Other preparations that use oils include creams, lotions, balms, and salves. The primary difference between each of these is the oil-to-water ratio. Creams use a base of approximately equal parts oil and water, while lotions use mostly water with a small amount of oil (and sometimes alcohol). Balms add ingredients like beeswax to reach a thick, near-solid consistency. Salves are similar again, but tend to be thinner than balms and thicker than ointments.

Many oil-based preparations have moisturising qualities that can soothe and hydrate the skin when applied to it directly. Moisturising treatments are referred to as emollients. Emollients don't need to be oil-based, however; gels are made from a base of water, alcohol, and cellulose, and are designed as a liniment treatment for people with oily skin types so they can use topical products without adding to their skin's natural oil content.

In addition to water and oil, plant-based medicines can also be delivered in an alcohol solution. Tinctures are made by dissolving plant matter in a mixture of ethanol and water. Typically, the ethanol to water concentration varies between 25%/75% to 60%/40%, but some tinctures are as high as 90%/10%. This variation can be based on the specific plants being used and the amount of alcohol required to extract the key medicinal components from the plant matter. The plant materials are steeped in this mixture for several weeks, before the solids are strained out of the liquid. The liquid preserves the components of the herb, and can be used as is or heated to burn off the alcohol before use.

All of these terms—poultices, tinctures, salves, and so on—tend to be associated with witches, naturopaths, and conspiracy theorists. But understanding what these words mean helps us see that many of the medications we are prescribed by the allopathic medical system or the home remedies our parents prepared for us are, at their core, herbal medicines. My grandfather, Kev, knows which plants are native and helping the environment, which are weeds taking nutrients from the other plants nearby, which are useful and can help us, and which are sick and need our help. He helped me pick lemon myrtle leaves from his tree when I was a kid and mix them in water, not just to create fantastical potions, but to make infusions that I could actually drink.

There are many ways to bring nature inside, from lemon myrtle tea to a handful of cowrie shells displayed in a glass jar. I didn't realise as a child how lucky I was to be allowed to bring icecream containers with caterpillars or grasshoppers into the house so I could watch them eat, grow, and change. While it's practical to understand which plants can nourish us and which can hurt us for our health, nutrition, and survival, it also feels magical to be able to identify the specific leaves, shells, or insects that we see in our daily lives. When we transition from seeing trees on the sidewalk to seeing oaks, poplars, and elms, we start to see the details that the Earth has created for us. Similarly, when we start to read the back of food containers or medicine boxes and understand which plants are listed—rather than becoming scared of the unfamiliar names of their phytochemicals—we are able to bridge the divide between our modern way of living and the natural world we are irrevocably connected to.

CONCLUSION

We exist in a complicated world. Media and online influencers, self-help and diet books, and sometimes even scientific researchers and medical doctors try to simplify it by giving us clear rules about what to eat, how to behave, what medicine to take, which gender roles to adhere to, and who to trust. Sometimes it's easier to let these messages motivate and manipulate us, because taking the time to reflect, research, and make decisions for ourselves is challenging—and *exhausting*.

This book started as a series of disconnected dot points I wrote as I tried to understand who I am, and who society wants me to be. I knew the basics of Western gender roles, the challenges of navigating the medical system as a marginalised person, and the beauty of the things that can be found in nature—but I wanted to know more. I wanted to know enough that I could connect the dots and make decisions. Not based on the black-and-white rules others were trying to convince me to follow, but based on my own instincts and wisdom.

The manuscript I ended up with is a time capsule of this part of my life as I enter my 30s understanding who I am with more clarity than the previous three decades of my life. But it also feels like a time capsule of this reality I'm living in, highlighting the triumphs and challenges of cynical people desperate to find purpose, vulnerable people desperate to achieve equitable human rights, chronically ill people desperate to find answers, neurodivergent people desperate to have agency over their treatment, and lonely people desperate to reconnect with each other and our planet.

The complexity of humanity's history is obvious when you consider anything with scrutiny. Every story comes with chaos and misconceptions, nuance and appropriation. Each community we join, tradition we practise, and scientific discovery we benefit from, seems to be surrounded by complications that are so exceptionally *human*. Gerald Gardner pretended to champion women's rights while forcing Doreen Valiente out of the organisation she helped him create; William Rider and Arthur Edward Waite erased Pamela Coleman Smith's name from the tarot deck that she so lovingly illustrated; our modern understanding of autism was founded by a literal Nazi sympathiser and a man who stole his work; Jérôme Lejeune allegedly failed to credit Marthe Gautier appropriately for her research; and Simon Baron-Cohen dismisses the expertise and lived experience of fellow scientists because he refuses to see how gender disparity is inherently political.

So much of what we consider enduring and constant is actually incredibly new: germ theory, nutritional science, fridges, vaccines, diagnoses like autism and ADHD, and the Universal Declaration of Human Rights. We are in a period of constant change and evolution, with people constantly claiming certainty over concepts we barely knew yesterday.

This is scary. But it's also *exciting*.

Because so much of what we consider enduring and constant *is*: we have been staring up at the same Moon for all of human history; we have been finding beautiful things in nature and bringing them into our homes forever; we have learned from nature and used her bounty to heal our maladies for as long as we've been getting sick; we have built things with our hands; we have created art; and we have loved each other.

Everything is incredibly complicated, but perhaps it's also incredibly simple.

I'm not perfect. Despite doing this research and composing this book, many of the realisations I've written here are still a work in progress. I still feel guilty, ashamed, or embarrassed about choices and mistakes that I know deserve self-compassion instead.

But this book is not an ending; it's the start of something.

It's a commitment to continue caring for others and myself in equal measure. It's a reminder to rest when my brain or body is having a bad day, to use the dishwasher when I want to, and to eat potatoes without judgement. It's a promise to return to the third spaces and find the people who wait for me there, friends and strangers alike. It's a realisation that I've been existing inside a cage but I've always had the key. It's a devotion to ignoring expectations, returning to the forest, and becoming wild.

Special Thanks

Dakoda, for your inspiring ideas, tireless encouragement, and reminders to eat on days that I'm trying to write. You're my favourite reader, editor, and supporter.

Sophie and Jessie, for being vital parts of my healthcare team and helping me understand my body, manage my pain, and forgive myself when I'm not at my best.

Liesl, for understanding me so quickly and helping me understand myself. Edwina, for continuing the work Liesl started.

Em, for teaching me how to be a better leader and a better person. Our conversations about art and witchcraft are a blessing.

My colleagues and friends—especially Jess, Amber, Isabelle, Shane, Mike, Char, Greg, and Carolyn—for tolerating my updates, sneak previews, celebrations, unavailability, countdowns, and complaints. Many of the conversations we've shared over the years found their way into these pages—and my life—in one way or another.

CITATIONS

1 Wang, W, He, W, Ruan, Y, et al. 2022. 'First pig-to-human heart transplantation' *Innovation (Camb)*. 3 (2): 100223.

2 Morwood, M. 2022. 'James Webb Space Telescope captures star-filled new images of the Pillars of Creation' *ABC*. Accessed 22 July 2023 from https://www.abc.net.au/news/2022-10-20/james-webb-telescope-new-images-pillars-of-creation/101555176

3 Blumenson, E. 2020. 'How are Human Rights Universal?' *Carr Center Discussion Paper Series*. 2020 (12).

4 Hough, A. 2022. 'The 120th anniversary of women's suffrage in Australia' *Parliament of Australia*. Accessed 22 October 2022 from https://www.aph.gov.au/About_Parliament/Parliamentary_Departments/Parliamentary_Library/FlagPost/2022/June/Womens_suffrage

5 National Museum Australia. n.d. 'Indigenous Australians' right to vote' *National Museum Australia*. Accessed 23 October 2022 from

https://www.nma.gov.au/defining-moments/
resources/indigenous-australians-right-to-vote

6 Inanici F and Yunus, M B. 2004. 'History of
fibromyalgia: past to present' *Curr Pain
Headache Rep.* 8 (5): 369-78.

7 ABC. 2015. 'Timeline: 22 years between first and
last Australian states decriminalising male
homosexuality' *ABC*. Accessed 23 October 2022
from https://www.abc.net.au/news/2015-08-24/
timeline:-australian-states-decriminalise-male-
homosexuality/6719702

8 Amnesty International. 2023. 'Amnesty
International Report 2022/23: The State of the
World's Human Rights' *Amnesty International*.
Accessed 29 July 2023 from https://www.
amnesty.org/en/wp-content/uploads/2023/03/
WEBPOL1056702023ENGLISH.pdf

9 Ryan, M. 2022. 'Human rights and democracy
eroding worldwide, U.S. finds' *The Washington
Post*. Accessed 29 July 2023 from https://
www.washingtonpost.com/national-
security/2022/04/12/state-global-human-rights-
report/

10 Schleien, D. 2020. 'Why You Should Reconnect
with Nature' *Medium*. Accessed 5 November
2022 from https://medium.com/climate-
conscious/why-you-should-reconnect-with-
nature-194b4453dbcb

11 Sinclair, M. 2019. 'Why the Self-Help Industry
Is Dominating the U.S.' *Medium*. Accessed 22
October 2022 from https://medium.com/s/story/
no-please-help-yourself-981058f3b7cf

12 Grand View Research. 2020. 'Personal
Development Market Size, Share & Trends

Analysis Report By Instrument (Books, e-Platforms, Personal Coaching/Training), By Focus Area, By Region, And Segment Forecasts, 2022 - 2030' *Grand View Research.* Accessed 22 October 2022 from https://www.grandviewresearch.com/industry-analysis/personal-development-market

[13] McCredie, J. 2022. 'Self-help industry more about narcissism than improvement' *InSight.* Accessed 22 October 2022 from https://insightplus.mja.com.au/2022/6/self-help-industry-more-about-narcissism-than-improvement/

[14] Gordon, A and Hobbes, M. 2020. 'Moon Juice'. *Maintenance Phase* Podcast. Accessed 30 October 2022 from https://maintenancephase.buzzsprout.com/1411126/6293911-moon-juice

[15] Eschner, K. 2017. 'Coca-Cola's Creator Said the Drink Would Make You Smarter' *Smithsonian Magazine.* Accessed 30 October 2022 from https://www.smithsonianmag.com/smart-news/coca-colas-creator-said-drink-would-make-you-smarter-180962665/

[16] Coca-Cola Company. 2022. 'Is it true that Coca-Cola started as a medicine?' *Coca-Cola Australia.* Accessed 30 October 2022 from https://www.coca-colacompany.com/au/faqs/is-it-true-that-coca-cola-started-as-a-medicine

[17] Markel, H. 2017. 'The remarkable history in your cereal bowl'. *CNN.* Accessed 30 October 2022 from https://edition.cnn.com/2017/08/13/health/kellogg-corn-flakes-wellness-history-markel/index.html

[18] Money, J. 1985. *The Destroying Angel: Sex, Fitness, & Food in the Legacy of Degeneracy Theory,* Graham

Crackers, Kellogg's Corn Flakes, & American Health History. New York: Prometheus Books.

[19] 'Kellogg, John Harvey' *The Eugenics Archives*. Accessed March 4, 2021.

[20] Byrne, R. 2006. *The Secret*. Hillsboro, OR: Atria Books / Beyond Words Publishing

[21] Winfrey, O. 2006. 'Discovering The Secret' *Oprah*. Accessed 31 October 2022 from https://www.oprah.com/spirit/_75

[22] Manson, M. 2016. *The Subtle Art of Not Giving a F*ck*. San Francisco, CA: HarperOne.

[23] MacMillan. 2022. 'The Subtle Art Of Not Giving A _ Journal' *MacMillan*. Accessed 31 October 2022 from https://www.panmacmillan.com.au/9781761261152/

[24] Bates, L. 2020. 'Incels, 'Men Going Their Own Way' And Pickup Artists: The Truth About Extreme Misogyny' *Elle*. Accessed 1 November 2022 from https://www.elle.com/uk/life-and-culture/a33831679/incels-men-who-hate-women/

[25] Hornsey, M J, Lobera, J, and Díaz-Catalán, C. 2020. 'Vaccine hesitancy is strongly associated with distrust of conventional medicine, and only weakly associated with trust in alternative medicine' *Social Science & Medicine*. 255: 113019.

[26] Trotta, S O. 2015. 'Want to Exercise Out of Self-Love and Not Self-Hate, But Have No Clue Where to Start? Try These 4 Suggestions' *Everyday Feminism*. Accessed 1 November 2022 from https://everydayfeminism.com/2015/05/exercising-out-of-self-love/

[27] Frick, W. 2014. 'Millennials Are Cynical Do-Gooders' *Harvard Business Review*. Accessed 1 November 2022 from https://hbr.org/2014/05/

millennials-are-cynical-do-gooders

[28] Haugh, M. 2011. 'Humour, face and im/politeness in getting acquainted' *Situated Politeness*. Davies, B L, Haugh, M, and Merrison, A J (eds). London, UK: Bloomsbury Publishing. 165-184.

[29] Schwartz, A. 2018. 'Improving ourselves to death: What the self-help gurus and the critics reveal about our times' *The New Yorker*. Accessed 22 October 2022 from https://www.newyorker.com/magazine/2018/01/15/improving-ourselves-to-death

[30] Renner, B. 2019. 'Survey: 2 in 3 millennials feel disconnected from their communities' *Study Finds*. Accessed 1 November 2022 from https://studyfinds.org/survey-most-millennials-feel-disconnected-community/

[31] Winerman, L. 2022. 'COVID-19 pandemic led to increase in loneliness around the world' *American Psychological Association*. Accessed 30 July 2023 from https://www.apa.org/news/press/releases/2022/05/covid-19-increase-loneliness

[32] Burgess, M and McKay, G. 2021. 'Melbourne Reopens, Ending One of World's Longest Lockdowns' *Bloomberg*. Accessed 30 July 2023 from https://www.bloomberg.com/news/articles/2021-10-21/one-of-world-s-longest-lockdowns-set-to-end-today-in-melbourne

[33] State Government of Victoria. 2023. 'Victorian COVID-19 data' *Coronavirus*. Accessed 30 July 2023 from https://www.coronavirus.vic.gov.au/victorian-coronavirus-covid-19-data

[34] Fialho M F P, Brum E S, and Oliveira S M. 2023. 'Could the fibromyalgia syndrome be triggered or enhanced by COVID-19?'

Inflammopharmacology. 31 (2): 633-651.

[35] Lewis R K, Martin P P, and Guzman B L. 2022. 'COVID-19 and vulnerable populations'. *J Community Psychol.* 50 (6): 2537-2541.

[36] Sanchez-Gomez M, Giorgi G, Finstad G L, et al. 2021. 'COVID-19 Pandemic as a Traumatic Event and Its Associations with Fear and Mental Health: A Cognitive-Activation Approach' *Int J Environ Res Public Health.* 18 (14): 7422.

[37] Migala, J. 2022. 'We're Increasingly Disconnected and That Has Consequences' *WebMD Health News.* Accessed 1 November 2022 from https://www.webmd.com/balance/news/20220916/increasingly-disconnected-consequences

[38] Oldenburg, R. 2002. *Celebrating the Third Place: Inspiring Stories About the "Great Good Places" at the Heart of Our Communities.* Cambridge, MA: Da Capo Press.

[39] AlibsWrites. 2023. 'The Death of Third Places and the Evolution of Communities' *Medium.* Accessed 2 August 2023 from https://medium.com/illumination/the-death-of-third-places-and-the-evolution-of-communities-5bbffc01c5e

[40] Kirman, A and Teschl, M. 2010. 'Selfish or selfless? The role of empathy in economics' *Philosophical Transactions of the Royal Society B: Biological Sciences.* 365 (1538): 303-317.

[41] Heinrich, T. 2013. 'When is foreign aid selfish, when is it selfless?' *The Journal of Politics.* 75 (2): 422-435.

[42] Layne, L L. 2020. *Selfishness and Selflessness: New Approaches to Understanding Morality.* New York, NY: Berghahn Books.

[43] Sonne, J W and Gash, D M. 2018. 'Psychopathy to

altruism: Neurobiology of the selfish–selfless spectrum'. *Frontiers in Psychology*. 9: 575.

44 Darbi, M, 2020. 'Applying the Concept of Voluntariness to Explain Behavior Towards Environmental Conservation' *Biodiversity Offsets Between Regulation and Voluntary Commitment*. New York, NY: Springer.

45 Bennett, J. 2022. 'Selfless Selfishness: The Me and We of Individuality' *Taboo: The Journal of Culture and Education*. 21 (1): 7.

46 Talkspace. 2019. '4 Therapists on What You Won't Get From Self-Help Books' *Talkspace*. Accessed 30 July 2023 from https://www.talkspace.com/blog/self-help-books-versus-therapy/

47 Andersen, B. 2022. 'Mastering Leadership' *The Leadership Circle*. Accessed 30 October 2022 from https://leadercircle.wpenginepowered.com/wp-content/uploads/2018/03/Mastering_Leadership.pdf

48 Mayo Clinic. 2022. 'Seasonal affective disorder (SAD)' *Mayo Clinic*. Accessed 5 November 2022 from https://www.mayoclinic.org/diseases-conditions/seasonal-affective-disorder/symptoms-causes/syc-20364651

49 Rosenthal, N E. 2009. 'Issues for DSM-V: Seasonal Affective Disorder and Seasonality' *The American Journal of Psychiatry*. 166 (8): 852-3.

50 Kesebir S and Kesebir P. 2017 'A Growing Disconnection From Nature Is Evident in Cultural Products' *Perspect Psychol Sci*. 12 (2): 258-269.

51 Bezin, E and Schumacher, I. 2020. 'What impacts do urbanization and nature disconnection have on environmental quality?' *Paris School*

of Economics. Accessed 5 November 2022 from https://www.parisschoolofeconomics.eu/en/economics-for-everybody/archives/5-papers-in-5-minutes/january-2020/what-impacts-do-urbanization-and-nature-disconnection-have-on-environmental-quality;

[52] Good, K. 2020. 'The Surprising Effect Being Disconnected From Nature Has on Our Health and Well-Being' *Our Green Planet.* Accessed 5 November 2022 from https://www.onegreenplanet.org/environment/natural-world-impact-on-human-health-and-well-being/

[53] Weir, K. 2020. 'Nurtured by nature' *Monitor on Psychology.* 51 (3): 50.

[54] Lee I, Choi H, Bang K S, et al. 2017. 'Effects of Forest Therapy on Depressive Symptoms among Adults: A Systematic Review' *Int J Environ Res Public Health.* 14 (3): 321.

[55] Louv, R. 2005. *Last Child in the Woods: Saving Our Children From Nature-Deficit Disorder.* Chapel Hill, NC: Algonquin Books.

[56] American Medical Association. 2020. '8 reasons patients don't take their medications' *American Medical Association.* Accessed 6 November 2022 from https://www.ama-assn.org/delivering-care/patient-support-advocacy/8-reasons-patients-dont-take-their-medications

[57] Brody, J E. 2017. 'The Cost of Not Taking Your Medicine' *New York Times.* Accessed 6 November 2022 from https://www.nytimes.com/2017/04/17/well/the-cost-of-not-taking-your-medicine.html

[58] Nourished Life. 2016. 'Mainstream Products

Can Disrupt Our Hormones' *Nourished Life*. Accessed 6 November 22 from https://www. nourishedlife.com.au/article/211787/mainstream-products-can-disrupt-our-hormones.html

59 Chemical Free Community. 2022. 'About our Community' *Chemical Free Community*. Accessed 6 November 2022 from http://www. chemfreecom.com/cfc-about/

60 Reeser, D. 2013. '"Chemical" Is Not a Bad Word' *Scientific American*. Accessed 6 November 2022 from https://blogs.scientificamerican.com/ guest-blog/chemical-is-not-a-bad-word/

61 NASA. 2016. '10 interesting things about air' *NASA*. Accessed 6 November 2022 from https://climate. nasa.gov/news/2491/10-interesting-things-about-air/

62 Poslusny, C. 2019. 'What is stale air? It's actually chemicals like CO2 and MVOCs' *Molekule*. Accessed 6 November 2022 from https:// molekule.com/blog/what-is-stale-air/

63 Brown, D. 2021. 'Think critically about avoiding chemicals - they are likely to save you at some point' *Wanted*. Accessed 6 November 2022 from https://www.wantedonline.co.za/wellness/2021-09-30-think-critically-about-avoiding-chemicals--they-are-likely-to-save-you-at-some-point/

64 Llor C and Bjerrum L. 2014. 'Antimicrobial resistance: risk associated with antibiotic overuse and initiatives to reduce the problem' *Ther Adv Drug Saf*. 5 (6): 229-41.

65 Lynch, S S. 2022. 'Tolerance and Resistance' *MSD Manual*. Accessed 12 November 2022 from https://www.msdmanuals.com/en-au/

professional/clinical-pharmacology/factors-
affecting-response-to-drugs/tolerance-and-
resistance

[66] The Sunlight Experiment. 2018. '9 Famous
Examples of Drugs That Came From Plants'
The Sunlight Experiment. Accessed 11 October
2021 from https://thesunlightexperiment.com/
blog/2018/6/7/9-famous-examples-of-drugs-
that-came-from-plants

[67] Stoeber, M, Jullié, D, Lobingier, B T, et al. 2018.
'A Genetically Encoded Biosensor Reveals
Location Bias of Opioid Drug Action' *Neuron.*
Accessed 30 October 2021 from https://www.nih.
gov/news-events/nih-research-matters/how-
opioid-drugs-activate-receptor

[68] Funnell, R. 2016. '5 drugs derived from plants' *The
English Garden.* Accessed 10 October 2021 from
https://www.theenglishgarden.co.uk/plants/5-
drugs-derived-from-plants/

[69] Turns, A. 2022. 'Are 'natural' products better than
synthetic ones?' *BBC.* Accessed 12 November
2022 from https://www.bbc.com/future/
article/20220614-synthetic-or-natural-which-is-
best-for-climate-and-health

[70] Harvard Library. 2022. 'Germ Theory' *Harvard
Library: Curiosity Collections.* Accessed 12
November 2022 from https://curiosity.lib.
harvard.edu/contagion/feature/germ-theory

[71] Lecoq H. 2001. 'Découverte du premier virus, le
virus de la mosaïque du tabac: 1892 ou 1898?
Discovery of the first virus, the tobacco mosaic
virus: 1892 or 1898?' *C R Acad Sci III.* 324 (10):
929-33.

[72] Strochlic, N. 2020. '"Wash your hands" was

once controversial medical advice' *National Geographic*. Accessed 4 Oct 2021 from https://www.nationalgeographic.com/history/article/handwashing-once-controversial-medical-advice

73 Faivre, A. 1994. *Access to Western Esotericism (SUNY Series in Western Esoteric Traditions)*. Albany, NY: SUNY Press.

74 Hanegraaff, W J. 'The notion of "occult sciences" in the wake of the Enlightenment' *Aufklärung und Esoterik: Wege in die Moderne*. Berlin, Germany: De Gruyter. 73-95.

75 Strube, J. 2019. 'Doesn't occultism lead straight to fascism?' *Hermes Explains: Thirty Questions about Western Esotericism*. Amsterdam, The Netherlands: Amsterdam University Press.

76 Kurlander, E. 2017. 'Hitler's Monsters: A Supernatural History of the Third Reich' *The Spectator*. Accessed 4 Oct 2021 from https://www.spectator.co.uk/article/nazis-and-the-dark-arts

77 Phillips, B. 2018. 'The Magical Thinking of the Far Right' *The Ringer*. Accessed 4 Oct 2021 from https://www.theringer.com/2018/12/12/18137221/far-right-occult-symbols

78 Garbedian, H G. 1929. 'The Star Stuff That Is Man' *New York Times*. 11 August 1929. New York;

79 Sagan C. 1973. *The Cosmic Connection: An Extraterrestrial Perspective*. Garden City, NY: Anchor Press.

80 Howell, E. 2017. 'Humans Really Are Made of Stardust, and a New Study Proves It' *Space*. Accessed 30 July 2023 from https://www.space.com/35276-humans-made-of-stardust-galaxy-

life-elements.html

81 Davies, O. 2011. *Paganism: a very short introduction.*
   Oxford, UK: Oxford University Press.

82 Strmiska, M. (ed) 2005. *Modern Paganism in World
   Cultures: Comparative Perspectives.* Santa Barbara,
   CA: ABC-CLIO.

83 Bonewits, I. 2006. *Bonewits's Essential Guide to
   Druidism* New York, NY: Kensington Publishing
   Corporation;

84 Bonewits, I. 2007. *Neopagan rites: A guide to
   creating public rituals that work.* Woodbury, MN:
   Llewellyn Worldwide.

85 Dundzila, V R. 2007. 'Baltic Lithuanian Religion
   and Romuva'. *Tyr: Myth, Culture, Tradition.* 3.

86 Gilmore, L. 2019. 'Pagan and Indigenous
   Communities in Interreligious Contexts:
   Interrogating Identity, Power, and Authenticity'.
   Pomegranate. 20 (2): 179–207.

87 Agrippa, Henry Cornelius (2021) 1531-33. *Three
   Books of Occult Philosophy.* Translated by Eric
   Purdue. Rochester, VT: Inner Traditions.

88 Willow. 2019. 'Bone magic series: A brief history
   of animal remains in magic' *Flying the Hedge.*
   Accessed 20 October 2022 from https://www.
   flyingthehedge.com/2019/02/bone-magic-series-
   brief-history-of.html

89 Chaucer, G. 2012. *The Canterbury Tales.* Ontario,
   Canada: Broadview Press.

90 Grimm, J. 2012. 1835. *Teutonic Mythology.* Translated
   by James Steven Stallybrass. Cambridge, UK:
   Cambridge University Press;

91 Richardson-Andrews, C. 2019. 'The pagan
   boom – why young people are turning to non-
   traditional religions' *Dazed Digital.* Accessed 23

July 2023 from https://www.dazeddigital.com/
life-culture/article/43242/1/the-pagan-boom-
young-people-non-traditional-religions-druids-
witchcraft

92 Danziger Halperin, A K. 2022. 'Witches are
having a moment in 2022' *The Washington
Post*. Accessed 30 July 2023 from https://
www.washingtonpost.com/made-by-
history/2022/10/31/witches-patriarchy-
halloween/

93 Marchetti, K. 2022. 'A Political Profile of U.S.
Pagans' *Politics and Religion*. 15 (1): 142-168.

94 Rudgley, Richard. 2007. *Pagan Resurrection: A
Force for Evil or the Future of Western Spirituality?*
London: Arrow Books.

95 Senholt, J C. 2013. 'Secret Identities in the
Sinister Tradition: Political Esotericism and
the Convergence of Radical Islam, Satanism,
and National Socialism in the Order of Nine
Angles' *The Devil's Party: Satanism in Modernity*.
Faxneld P and Petersen J A (eds). Oxford, UK:
Oxford University Press. 250–274.

96 Birkett, T. 2021. 'US Capitol riot: the myths
behind the tattoos worn by 'QAnon shaman'
Jake Angeli' *The Conversation*. Accessed 30
July 2023 from https://theconversation.com/
us-capitol-riot-the-myths-behind-the-tattoos-
worn-by-qanon-shaman-jake-angeli-152996

97 Williams, M M. 2017. '"Celtic" Crosses and White
Supremacism' *The Material Collective*. Accessed
30 July 2023 from http://thematerialcollective.
org/celtic-crosses-white-supremacism/

98 ADL. 2023. 'Hate on Display™ Hate Symbols
Database' *Anti-Defamation League*. Accessed 30

July 2023 from https://www.adl.org/resources/hate-symbols/search

99 McMaster, G. 2020. 'White supremacists are misappropriating Norse mythology, says expert' *University of Alberta: Folio.* Accessed 30 July 2023 from https://www.ualberta.ca/folio/2020/07/white-supremacists-are-misappropriating-norse-mythology-says-expert.html

100 United States Holocaust Memorial Museum. 2017. 'History of the Swastika' *United States Holocaust Memorial Museum.* Accessed 30 July 2023 from https://encyclopedia.ushmm.org/content/en/article/history-of-the-swastika

101 Adler, M. 2006. 1979. *Drawing Down the Moon: Witches, Druids, Goddess-Worshippers, and Other Pagans in America Today.* London, UK: Penguin Books.

102 Jones, P, and Pennick, N. 1995. *A History of Pagan Europe.* Milton Park, UK: Routledge.

103 BBC 2. 2015. *The Celts Blood Iron And Sacrifice With Alice Roberts And Neil Oliver.* TV miniseries

104 The Clan Buchanan Society International. 2022. 'Religion in Scotland' *The Clan Buchanan.* Accessed 30 July 2023 from https://www.theclanbuchanan.com/religion-spirituality

105 Pliny the Elder. *Natural History.* 79 1945. Volume IV: Books 12-16. Translated by H. Rackham. Loeb Classical Library 370. Cambridge, MA: Harvard University Press.

106 McKillop, J. 1998. 'Hazel' *A Dictionary of Celtic Mythology.* Oxford, UK: Oxford University Press.

107 Shurpin, Y. 2017. 'Why Do Jews Put Stones on Graves?' *Chabad-Lubavitch Media Center.* Accessed 30 July 2023 from https://www.chabad.

org/library/article_cdo/aid/3002484/jewish/
Why-Do-Jews-Put-Pebbles-on-Tombstones.
htm;

[108] McGuire, E. 2017. 'Stones On Jewish Monuments-
A Symbolic Praxis (Guest post by Morgan and
Basil)' *University of Victoria*. Accessed 30 July
2023 from https://onlineacademiccommunity.
uvic.ca/archaeograves/2017/05/27/stones-on-
jewish-monuments-a-symbolic-praxis-guest-
post-by-morgan-and-basil/

[109] Cartwright, M. 2021. 'Sacred Sites & Rituals
in the Ancient Celtic Religion' *World History
Encyclopedia*. Accessed 30 July 2023 from https://
www.worldhistory.org/article/1710/sacred-sites--
rituals-in-the-ancient-celtic-religi/

[110] Cartwright, M. 2021. 'Death, Burial & the Afterlife
in the Ancient Celtic Religion' *World History
Encyclopedia*. Accessed 30 July 2023 from https://
www.worldhistory.org/article/1707/death-burial-
-the-afterlife-in-the-ancient-celtic/

[111] Cartwright, M. 2021. 'Ancient Celtic Sculpture'
World History Encyclopedia. Accessed 30 July 2023
from https://www.worldhistory.org/Ancient_
Celtic_Sculpture/;

[112] Cartwright, M. 2021. 'Celtic Coinage' *World History
Encyclopedia*. Accessed 30 July 2023 from https://
www.worldhistory.org/Celtic_Coinage/

[113] de Greef, K and Seelie, T. 2020. 'The White Sage
Black Market' *Vice*. Accessed 31 July 2023 from
https://www.vice.com/en/article/m7jkma/the-
white-sage-black-market-v27n3

[114] Forage and Sustain. 2019. 'Why We Need to Stop
Using Palo Santo' *Forage and Sustain*. Accessed
31 July 2023 from https://forageandsustain.com/

why-we-need-to-stop-using-palo-santo/

[115] Karim, N. n.d. 'Dreamcatchers are not your 'aesthetic" *The Indigenous Foundation.* Accessed 31 July 2023 from https://www. theindigenousfoundation.org/articles/ dreamcatchers

[116] MexLocal. 2021. 'Mexican Cultural Appropriation: Is Day of the Dead Makeup Inappropriate?' *MexLocal.* Accessed 31 July 2023 from https:// mexlocal.com/mexican-cultural-appropriation- day-of-the-dead-makeup/

[117] Doyle White, E. 2010. 'The Meaning of "Wicca": A Study in Etymology, History and Pagan Politics' *The Pomegranate: The International Journal of Pagan Studies.* 12 (2): 185–207.

[118] Pasi, M. 2007. 'Occultism' in von Stuckrad, K (ed). *The Brill Dictionary of Religion.* Leiden and Boston: Brill Publishers.

[119] Blavatsky, H. 1875. 'A Few Questions to 'Hiraf".

[120] Hanegraaff, W. 2013. 'Western Esotericism: A Guide for the Perplexed' *Guides for the Perplexed.* London, UK: Bloomsbury Press.

[121] Rose, E. 1962. *A Razor for a Goat: A Discussion of Certain Problems in Witchcraft and Diabolism.* Toronto: Toronto University Press;

[122] Cohn, N. 1975. *Europe's Inner Demons: An Enquiry Inspired by the Great Witch-Hunt.* Sussex and London: Sussex University Press and Heinemann Educational Books;

[123] Ginzburg, C. 1983 1966. *The Night Battles: Witchcraft and Agrarian Cults in the Sixteenth and Seventeenth Centuries.* John and Anne Tedeschi (translators). Baltimore: Johns Hopkins Press;

[124] Thomas, K. 1971. *Religion and the Decline of*

Magic: Studies in Popular Beliefs in Sixteenth and Seventeenth Century England. London: Weidenfeld & Nicolson.

[125] Simpson, J. 1994. 'Margaret Murray: Who Believed Her, and Why?' *Folklore.* 105 (1-2): 89-96.

[126] McHenry, T. 2020. *Occult Tarot.* Summer Hill, NSW: Rockpool Publishing.

[127] Kelly, A. 1991. *Crafting the Art of Magic, Book I: A History of Witchcraft, 1939–1964.* St Paul, Minnesota: Llewellyn;

[128] Ruickbie, L. 2004. *Witchcraft Out of the Closet: A Complete History.* London: Robert Hale;

[129] Hutton, R. 1999. *The Triumph of the Moon: A History of Modern Pagan Witchcraft.* New York: Oxford University Press.

[130] Heselton, P. 2003. *Gerald Gardner and the Cauldron of Inspiration: An Investigation into the Sources of Gardnerian Witchcraft.* Milverton, Somerset, UK: Capall Bann.

[131] Clifton, C S. 2014. 'Sex Magic or Sacred Marriage? Sexuality in Contemporary Wicca' *Sexuality and New Religious Movements.* Palgrave Macmillan, New York. 149-163.

[132] Burke, V. 2013. 'Recent Studies in Commonplace Books' *English Literary Renaissance.* 43 (1): 154.

[133] Valiente, D. 1989. *The Rebirth of Witchcraft.* London: Robert Hale.

[134] Valiente, D. 2000. *The Charge of the Goddess.* Hexagon Hoopix.

[135] Shuler, E. 2012. 'A balancing act: a discussion of gender roles within Wiccan ritual' *Intermountain West Journal of Religious Studies.* 4 (1): 3.

[136] Gardner, G. 1961. *The Gardnerian Book of Shadows: The Complete Wicca Initiations and Pagan Ritual*

Lore. Pantianos Classics.

[137] Worth, R. 2017. 'Witch Hunt' *The Overtake*. Accessed 1 Jan 2022 from https://theovertake. com/~alpha/wicca-sexual-predators/

[138] Frost, G and Frost, Y. 1972. *The Witch's Bible*. Nash Pub.

[139] Saxena, J. 2015. 'There's a Sexism Problem in the Modern Witchcraft Community' *Mic*. Accessed 1 Jan 2021 from https://www.mic.com/ articles/128928/there-s-a-sexism-problem-in-the-modern-witchcraft-community

[140] Rice, J A. 2012. 'Salem's official witch moves her magic online' *The Boston Globe*. Accessed 20 October 2022 from http://www.boston.com/ yourtown/salem/articles/2012/02/09/laurie_ cabot_salems_official_witch_closes_up_shop_ after_40_years/

[141] Malita-Król, J. 2021. 'On Choosing the Place: The Open Wiccan Rituals in the City of Warsaw' *Nova Religio*. 25 (1): 108-121.

[142] Marquis, M. 2015. *Beltane: Rituals, Recipes & Lore for May Day*. Woodbury, MN: Llewellyn Publications.

[143] Mark, J J. 2019. 'Wheel of the Year'. *World History Encyclopedia*. Accessed 23 July 2023 from https:// www.worldhistory.org/Wheel_of_the_Year/

[144] Grovier, K. 2019. 'The Moon: One of the earliest human symbols' *BBC Culture*. Accessed 28 May 2023 from https://www.bbc.com/culture/ article/20190326-the-moon-one-of-the-earliest-human-symbols

[145] Royal Museum Greenwich. n.d. 'Why do we have special names for full moons?' *Royal Museum Greenwich*. Accessed 28 May 2023 from https://

www.rmg.co.uk/stories/topics/what-are-names-full-moons-throughout-year

[146] Decker, R and Dummett, M. 2013. *The History of the Occult Tarot.* Hertfordshire, UK: Prelude Books.

[147] Challis, D J. 2011. 'Tarot and Ancient Egypt - A Connection?' *UCL Culture Blog.* Accessed 31 August 2022 from https://blogs.ucl.ac.uk/museums/2011/04/27/tarot-and-ancient-egypt-a-connection/

[148] Blavatsky, H P. 1895. *The Secret Doctrine: The synthesis of science, religion and philosophy* (vol 3). Theosophical Publishing Society.

[149] Said, E. 1978. *Orientalism.* New York: Vintage;

[150] Kamiya, G. 2006. 'How Edward said took intellectuals for a ride' *Salon.* Accessed 28 April 2020 from https://www.salon.com/2006/12/06/orientalism/

[151] Smith Galer, S. 2019. 'How art created stereotypes of the Arab world' *BBC.* Accessed 28 April 2020 from https://www.bbc.com/culture/article/20191017-how-art-created-stereotypes-of-the-arab-world

[152] Wilkinson, W H. 1895. 'Chinese Origin of Playing Cards' *American Anthropologist.* 8 (1): 61–78.

[153] Dummett, M. 1980. *The Game of Tarot.* London, UK: Duckworth.

[154] Poilly, F D. n.d. 'Jeu de minchiate de fantaisie à enseignes' *Gallica: Digital library of Bibliothèque nationale de France (BnF).* Accessed 23 July 2023 from françaiseshttps://gallica.bnf.fr/ark:/12148/btv1b103365240.item

[155] de Gébelin, A C. 1781. *The Primitive World, analyzed and compared with the modern world* (vol 8).

Translated by Donald Tyson. Unpublished.

[156] Oatman-Stanford, H. 2014. 'Tarot Mythology: The Surprising Origins of the World's Most Misunderstood Cards' *Collectors Weekly*. Accessed 28 May 2023 from https://www.collectorsweekly.com/articles/the-surprising-origins-of-tarot-most-misunderstood-cards

[157] bunnypudding. 2021. 'Is Tarot a closed practice? A Concise History of Tarot and Cartomancy' *Digital Coven*. Accessed 31 July 2023 from https://digital-coven.com/2021/01/25/is-tarot-a-closed-practice-a-concise-history-of-tarot-and-cartomancy/

[158] Dann, K. 2022. 'A Renaissance Riddle: The Sola Busca Tarot Deck (1491)' *The Public Domain Review*. Accessed 23 July 2023 from https://publicdomainreview.org/collection/sola-busca/

[159] Katz, M and Goodwin, T. 2015. *Secrets of the Waite-Smith Tarot*. Woodbury, MN: Llewellyn Publications.

[160] Dixon, J. 2001. *Divine Feminine: Theosophy and Feminism in England*. Baltimore, MD: JHU Press.

[161] Topolsky, L J. 2015. 'The Deck of Cards That Made Tarot A Global Phenomenon' *Atlas Obscura*. Accessed 23 July 2023 from https://www.atlasobscura.com/articles/the-deck-of-cards-that-made-tarot-a-global-phenomenon

[162] Melton, J G. 2023. 'Realizing the New Age' *Britannica*. Accessed 23 July 2023 from https://www.britannica.com/topic/New-Age-movement/Realizing-the-New-Age

[163] Semetsky, I. 2005. 'Integrating Tarot readings into counselling and psychotherapy' *Spirituality and Health International*. 6 (2): 81-94.

164 Teyber, E. 1992. *Interpersonal process in psychotherapy: A guide for clinical training.* Pacific Grove, CA: Thomson Brooks, Cole Publishing Co.

165 Auger, E. 2014. *Tarot and Other Meditation Decks: History, Theory, Aesthetics, Typology.* Jefferson, NC: McFarland.

166 Australian Government. 2022. 'Evaluation of the National School Chaplaincy Program' *Department of Education.* Accessed 31 July 2023 from https://www.education.gov.au/national-student-wellbeing-program-nswp/resources/2022-national-school-chaplaincy-programme-evaluation-report

167 Beck, L. 2022. 'To give schools real choice about secular school chaplains, latest change needs to go further' *The Conversation.* Accessed 31 July 2023 from https://theconversation.com/to-give-schools-real-choice-about-secular-school-chaplains-latest-change-needs-to-go-further-185487

168 National School Chaplaincy Association. 2017. 'Correcting Myths about School Chaplaincy' *National School Chaplaincy Association.* Accessed 31 July 2023 from https://schoolchaplaincy.org.au/wp-content/uploads/2018/04/NSCA-FACTSHEET-2018.pdf

169 Martin, K, Berger, E, and Kasten-Lee, M. 2020. 'School chaplains may be cheaper than psychologists. But we don't have enough evidence of their impact' *The Conversation.* Accessed 1 August 2023 from https://theconversation.com/school-chaplains-may-be-cheaper-than-psychologists-but-we-dont-have-

enough-evidence-of-their-impact-148521
[170] Shepherd, T. 2023. 'ADF has 108 evangelical chaplains with each representing just 15 members' *The Guardian*. Accessed 1 August 2023 from https://www.theguardian.com/australia-news/2023/jul/30/adf-has-108-evangelical-chaplains-with-each-representing-just-15-members
[171] Multifaith Chaplaincy. 2020. 'The Pagan as a Professional Chaplain' *Multifaith Chaplaincy*. Accessed 31 July 2023 from https://www.multifaithchaplaincy.org.au/2020/11/24/the-pagan-as-a-professional-chaplain/
[172] Muzyka, K. 2017. 'How a Wiccan chaplain helps U of A students with their mental health' *CBC News*. Accessed 1 August 2023 from https://www.cbc.ca/news/canada/edmonton/university-alberta-wicca-pagan-chaplain-1.4432929
[173] Wagar, S. 2020. 'Polytheist Among the Atheists: Reflections of a Wiccan University Chaplain' *Multifaith Perspectives in Spiritual and Religious Care*. Toronto, Canada: Canadian Multifaith Federation.
[174] Fowler, J. 2023. 'Multi-faith and belief chaplaincy, for all faiths and none' *The University of Edinburgh*. Accessed 1 August 2023 from https://www.ed.ac.uk/chaplaincy/about/staff-and-team/honorary-chaplains/pagan
[175] Jones, A. 2018. 'Wanted: pagan chaplains for Britain's prisons' *The Guardian*. Accessed 1 August 2023 from https://www.theguardian.com/society/shortcuts/2018/feb/28/wanted-pagan-chaplains-for-britains-prisons
[176] Isley, W. 2021. 'The Perils of a Pagan Hospital

Chaplain in a Christian World' *Rev. Wes Isley: Interfaith and Pagan Minister.* Accessed 1 August 2023 from https://www.revwesisley.com/post/the-perils-of-a-pagan-hospital-chaplain-in-a-christian-world

177 Pagan Chaplains Association. 2023. *Pagan Chaplains Association.* Accessed 1 August 2023 from http://www.paganchaplainsassociation.org/

178 Willis, J. 2012. 'The Plight of Pagans in the Military' *Religion and Politics.* Accessed 1 August 2023 from https://religionandpolitics.org/2012/06/20/the-plight-of-pagans-in-the-military/;

179 Cooperman, A. 2007. 'A Wiccan Army chaplain? The brass wouldn't buy it' *The Seattle Times.* Accessed 1 August 2023 from https://www.seattletimes.com/nation-world/a-wiccan-army-chaplain-the-brass-wouldnt-buy-it/

180 Banerjee, N. 2007. 'Use of Wiccan Symbol on Veterans' Headstones Is Approved'. *The New York Times.* Accessed 1 August 2023 from https://www.nytimes.com/2007/04/24/washington/24wiccan.html?_r=0

181 Schulz, C. 2017. 'Update to army religious codes' *The Wild Hunt.* Accessed 1 August 2023 from https://wildhunt.org/2017/04/department-of-defense-adds-heathen-and-pagan-religions-to-recognized-faith-groups.html

182 Stanton, K J. 2022. *BOTANICA: The Herbalist's Tarot.* Philadelphia, PA: Beehive Books.

183 Kott, M L. 2019. *Cat Tarot.* San Francisco, CA: Chronicle Books;

184 Cullinane, M J. 2023. *Grimalkin's Curious Cats Tarot.*

Carlsbad, CA: Hay House;

[185] Gilly, C and Mountford, K J. 2023. *Buffy the Vampire Slayer Tarot Deck and Guidebook.* San Rafael, CA: Insight Editions.

[186] Ari. 2022. 'Notes for a Queer Homemaker: States of Being, Not Moral Designations' *Autostraddle.* Accessed 28 May 2023 from https://www.autostraddle.com/notes-for-a-queer-homemaker-states-of-being-not-moral-designations

[187] Gordon, A and Hobbes, M. 2021. 'The Great Protein Fiasco' *Maintenance Phase* Podcast. Accessed 30 October 2022 from https://maintenancephase.buzzsprout.com/1411126/9114227-the-great-protein-fiasco

[188] Dewey, C. 2014. 'Everyone on the Internet does Venn diagrams wrong' *The Washington Post.* Accessed 28 May 2023 from https://www.washingtonpost.com/news/the-intersect/wp/2014/08/04/everyone-on-the-internet-does-venn-diagrams-wrong/

[189] Mozaffarian, D, Rosenberg, I, and Uauy, R. 2018. 'History of modern nutrition science—implications for current research, dietary guidelines, and food policy' *Science and Politics of Nutrition.* Accessed 28 May 2023 from https://www.bmj.com/content/361/bmj.k2392

[190] Nagler, R H. 2013. 'Adverse outcomes associated with media exposure to contradictory nutrition messages' *J Health Commun.* 19 (1) 24-40.

[191] Gordon, A and Hobbes, M. 2022. 'Calorie Menu Labeling' *Maintenance Phase* Podcast Accessed 28 May 2023 from https://maintenancephase.buzzsprout.com/1411126/10743798-calorie-menu-

labeling
192 Gordon, A and Hobbes, M. 2022. 'The
    Trouble with Calories' *Maintenance Phase*
    Podcast Accessed 28 May 2023 from
    https://maintenancephase.buzzsprout.
    com/1411126/10671811-the-trouble-with-calories
193 Gordon, A and Hobbes, M. 2022. 'The Food
    Pyramid' *Maintenance Phase* Podcast Accessed
    28 May 2023 from https://maintenancephase.
    buzzsprout.com/1411126/11690180-the-food-
    pyramid
194 Oxford University Press USA. 2022. 'Research
    Shows: Weight Loss Advice From Doctors Is
    Ineffective' *SciTechDaily*. Accessed 1 August 2023
    from https://scitechdaily.com/research-shows-
    weight-loss-advice-from-doctors-is-ineffective/
195 Sugar, R. 2019. 'How did home cooking
    become a moral issue?' *Vox*. Accessed 19
    October 2021 from https://www.vox.com/the-
    goods/2019/3/5/18250471/home-cooking-moral-
    pressure-cooker
196 Samadder, R. 2015. 'Kitchen gadgets review:
    the egg cuber – a medieval torture device to
    terrify hens' *The Guardian*. Accessed 1 August
    2023 from https://www.theguardian.com/
    lifeandstyle/2015/may/06/kitchen-gadgets-
    review-egg-cuber-square-eggs-medieval-
    torture-device
197 Fallen Solutions. 2018. 'A brief history of
    appliances' *Fallen Solutions*. Accessed 10 October
    2019 from https://www.fallonsolutions.com.au/
    handy-hints/a-brief-history-of-appliances
198 University of Montreal. 2009. 'Fridges and
    washing machines liberated women, study

suggests'. *ScienceDaily*. Accessed 19 October 2021 from https://www.sciencedaily.com/releases/2009/03/090312150735.htm

199 Kinsey, F. 2009. 'Selling Electricity to the Home' *Museums Victoria Collections*. https://collections.museumsvictoria.com.au/articles/2837 Accessed 28 May 2023;

200 Melbourne Water. 2022. 'History of our water supply system' *Melbourne Water*. Accessed 28 May 2023 from https://www.melbournewater.com.au/about/who-we-are/history-and-heritage/history-our-water-supply-system

201 Gross, R. 2005. 'Recipe for Success: A History of the Modern Australian Kitchen' *Houzz*. Accessed 28 May 2023 from https://www.houzz.com.au/magazine/recipe-for-success-a-history-of-the-modern-australian-kitchen-stsetivw-vs~48528894

202 Fiore, J. 2020. 'Reclaiming the Kitchen' *MoMA Magazine*. Accessed 19 October 2021 from https://www.moma.org/magazine/articles/240

203 Melching, K. 2006. 'Frankfurt Kitchen: Patina Follows Function' *Victoria and Albert Museum*. Accessed 18 December 2009 from http://www.vam.ac.uk/res_cons/conservation/journal/number_53/frankfurt/index.html

204 Marusic, K. 2016. People Still Believe Women Belong in the Kitchen and Men Belong at the Office' *Women's Health*. Accessed 1 August 2023 from https://www.womenshealthmag.com/life/a19934409/gender-stereotypes-study/

205 Grossman, A S. 1980. 'Women in domestic work: yesterday and today' *Monthly Labor Review*. 103 (8): 17-21.

[206] Higman, B. 2002. *Domestic Service in Australia.* Melbourne, VIC: Melbourne University Press.

[207] Power, L. 2012. 'When domesticity began at home' *Sydney Morning Herald.* Accessed 19 October 2021 from https://www.smh.com.au/entertainment/when-domesticity-began-at-home-20120803-23k96.html

[208] Levin, I. 1972. *The Stepford Wives.* New York, NY: Random House.

[209] McCarthy, H. 2020. 'The Rise of the Working Wife' *History Today.* 70 (5). Accessed 20 October 2021 from https://www.historytoday.com/history-matters/rise-working-wife

[210] Greenwood, J. 2019. *Evolving Households: The Imprint of Technology on Life.* Cambridge, MA: The MIT Press.

[211] Torrella, K. 2022. 'The environmental limits of eating local' *Vox.* Accessed 1 August 2023 from https://www.vox.com/future-perfect/23132579/eat-local-csa-farmers-markets-locavore-slow-food

[212] Levermann, A. 2019. 'Individuals can't solve the climate crisis. Governments need to step up' *The Guardian.* Accessed 1 August 2023 from https://www.theguardian.com/commentisfree/2019/jul/10/individuals-climate-crisis-government-planet-priority

[213] Brasted, C. 2021. 'Why cooking and baking fill a void' *BBC.* Accessed 1 August 2023 from https://www.bbc.com/worklife/article/20210128-why-cooking-and-baking-fills-a-void

[214] Cowan, R S. 1983. *More Work for Mother: The Ironies of Household Technology from the Open Hearth to the Microwave.* New York, NY: Basic Books.

215 Bilyeu, M. 2019. 'African-American culinary history includes role of cornbread' *The Blade*. Accessed 28 October 2021 from https://www.toledoblade.com/a-e/food/2019/02/04/cornbread-played-integral-role-in-african-american-history/stories/20190205004

216 Jack, S. 2017. 'Sydney Flour Mills before 1850' *The Dictionary of Sydney*. Accessed 29 May 2023 from https://dictionaryofsydney.org/entry/sydney_flour_mills_before_1850

217 Scott, C. 2019. 'America's Essential Connection to Cornbread' *Diced*. Accessed 28 October 2021 from https://www.ice.edu/blog/americas-cornbread-history

218 Ó Gráda, C. 1993. *Ireland before and after the Famine: Explorations in Economic History 1800–1925.* Manchester, UK: Manchester University Press

219 Ross, D. 2002. *Ireland: History of a Nation.* New Lanark, Scotland: Geddes & Grosset

220 Donnelly, J. 2011. 'British History in depth: The Irish Famine' *BBC History*. Accessed 2 August 2023 from https://www.bbc.co.uk/history/british/victorians/famine_01.shtml

221 Earle, R. 2020. 'The Politics of the Potato' *Feeding the People*. Cambridge, UK: Cambridge University Press. 140-167.

222 Beals, K A. 2019. 'Potatoes, Nutrition and Health' *American Journal of Potato Research* 96: 102-110;

223 Love Potatoes. 2019. 'Potato myths debunked' *Love Potatoes* Accessed 28 October 2021 from https://lovepotatoes.com.au/potato-myths-debunked/;

224 Hearne, A. 2019. 'Potato myths, busted!' *Easy Food* Accessed 28 October 2021 from https://easyfood.

ie/kitchen_tips/potato-myths-busted/

[225] Astrup, A, Larsen, T M, and Harper, A. 2004. 'Atkins and other low-carbohydrate diets: hoax or an effective tool for weight loss?' *The Lancet.* 364 (9437): 897-899.

[226] Hobbes, M and Marshall, S. 2020. 'The Stepford Wives' *You're Wrong About* Podcast Accessed 19 October 2021 from https://open.spotify.com/episode/7KF7jiyYyBWKhm9ybqyb3h;

[227] BBC. 2014. 'Rotary egg beater'. *A History of the World.* Accessed 21 October 2021 from https://www.bbc.co.uk/ahistoryoftheworld/objects/seWkoO7hT326RgsueSJtdz

[228] Lincoln, M J B. 1884. Boston Cooking School Cook Book. Boston, MA: Roberts Brothers.

[229] NRDC. 2016. '9 Tricks That Save Tons of Water' *Natural Resources Defense Council.* Accessed 1 August 2023 from https://www.nrdc.org/stories/9-tricks-save-tons-water

[230] Furie, M. 2018. 'Spell: Magical Dishwashing' *Llewellyn.* Accessed 1 August 2023 from https://www.llewellyn.com/spell.php?spell_id=7278

[231] Cherney, K, Holland, K, and Watson, S. 2022. 'Fibromyalgia' *Healthline.* Accessed 2 August 2023 from https://www.healthline.com/health/fibromyalgia

[232] Wolfe, F, Clauw, D J, Fitzcharles, M, et al. 2016. '2016 Revisions to the 2010/2011 fibromyalgia diagnostic criteria' *Seminars in arthritis and rheumatism,* 46 (3): 319-329.

[233] Qureshi A G, Jha S K, Iskander J, et al. 2021. 'Diagnostic Challenges and Management of Fibromyalgia' *Cureus.* 13 (10): e18692.

[234] Berenson, A. 2008. 'Drug Approved. Is Disease

Real?' *The New York Times.* Accessed 14 May 2022 from https://www.nytimes.com/2008/01/14/health/14pain.html

[235] American Psychiatric Association. 1980. *Diagnostic and Statistical Manual of Mental Disorders* (3rd ed). Washington DC, WA: American Psychiatric Association;

[236] Inanici F and Yunus, MB. 2004. 'History of fibromyalgia: past to present' *Curr Pain Headache Rep.* 8 (5): 369-78.

[237] Hauser, W and Fitzcharles, M A. 2018. 'Facts and myths pertaining to fibromyalgia'. *Dialogues Clin Neurosci* 20 (1): 53-62.

[238] American Psychiatric Association. 2022. *Diagnostic and Statistical Manual of Mental Disorders - Text Revision.* (5th ed.) Washington DC, WA: American Psychiatric Association.

[239] American Psychiatric Association. 2000. *Diagnostic and Statistical Manual of Mental Disorders - Text Revision.* (4th ed.) Washington DC, WA: American Psychiatric Association;

[240] American Psychiatric Association. 2013. 'Highlights of Changes from DSM-IV-TR to DSM-5' *American Psychiatric Association.* Accessed 14 May 2022 from https://www.psychiatry.org/File%20Library/Psychiatrists/Practice/DSM/APA_DSM_Changes_from_DSM-IV-TR_-to_DSM-5.pdf;

[241] Cohut, M. 2020. 'The controversy of 'female hysteria'. *Medical News Today.* Accessed 14 May 2020 from https://www.medicalnewstoday.com/articles/the-controversy-of-female-hysteria

[242] Tucker, A. 2009. 'History of the Hysterical Man' *Smithsonian Magazine.* Accessed 2 August

2023 from https://www.smithsonianmag.com/
science-nature/history-of-the-hysterical-
man-43321905/

[243] Holmes, T T. 2016. 'Tropical Storms Were Once
Named After Wives, Girlfriends, and Disliked
Politicians' *Atlas Obscura*. Accessed 29 May 2023
from https://www.atlasobscura.com/articles/
tropical-storms-were-once-named-after-wives-
girlfriends-and-disliked-politicians

[244] Little, B. 2020. 'Why Hurricanes and Tropical
Storms Were Only Named After Women'
History. Accessed 29 May 2023 from https://
www.history.com/news/why-hurricanes-and-
tropical-storms-were-only-named-after-women

[245] McElroy, S and McElroy, J. 2013. 'Hysteria'
Sawbones: A Marital Tour of Misguided Medicine
Podcast Maximum Fun. https://maximumfun.
org/episodes/sawbones/sawbones-hysteria/

[246] Mankiller, W P. 1998. *The Reader's Companion to
U.S. Women's History*. Boston, MA: Houghton
Mifflin Co.

[247] Tasca, C, Mariangela R, Mauro G C, et al. 2012.
'Women and Hysteria in the History of Mental
Health' *Clin Pract Epidemiol Ment Health*. 8: 110-
119.

[248] Gilman, S. 1993. *Hysteria Beyond Freud*. Berkeley,
CA: University of California Press. 18–20.

[249] McVean, A. 2017. 'The History of Hysteria' *McGill
Office for Science and Society*. Accessed 7 May
2022 from https://www.mcgill.ca/oss/article/
history-quackery/history-hysteria

[250] Russell, J B. 1972. *Witchcraft in the Middle Ages*.
Ithaca, NY: Cornell University Press.

[251] Lowth, M. 2017. 'Does torture work? Donald

Trump and the CIA' *Br J Gen Pract.* 67 (656): 126.

[252] Sluka, K A and Clauw, D J. 2016. 'Neurobiology of fibromyalgia and chronic widespread pain'. *Neuroscience.* 338: 114–129. https://doi.org/10.1016/j.neuroscience.2016.06.006

[253] William, A. 2022. 'The Medical Medium—and What's Potentially at the Root of Medical Mysteries' *Goop.* Accessed 20 May 2022 from https://goop.com/wellness/health/the-medical-medium-and-whats-potentially-at-the-root-of-medical-mysteries/

[254] Medical Medium. 2019. '12 Foods That Help Heal Epstein-Barr Virus' *Medical Medium.* Accessed 20 May 2022 from https://www.medicalmedium.com/blog/12-foods-that-help-heal-epstein-barr-virus

[255] Faguy, A. 2021. 'Fact check: No, celery juice will not help heal fibromyalgia' *USA Today* Accessed 24 November 2023 from https://www.usatoday.com/story/news/factcheck/2022/05/31/fact-check-no-celery-juice-not-help-heal-fibromyalgia/9823636002/

[256] Lehava, N. 2019. 'Is It Time to Stop Drinking Celery Juice?' *Coveteur* Accessed 24 November 2023 from https://coveteur.com/2019/01/28/truth-about-celery-juice-trend/

[257] Rush. 2022. 'The Truth About Toxins' *Rush.* Accessed 20 May 2022 from https://www.rush.edu/news/truth-about-toxins

[258] McCartney, G, Hearty, W, Arnot, J, et al. 2019. 'Impact of Political Economy on Population Health: A Systematic Review of Reviews'. *Am J Public Health.* 109 (6): e1-e12.

[259] McElroy, S and McElroy, J. 2015. 'Lyme Disease'

Sawbones: A Marital Tour of Misguided Medicine Podcast Maximum Fun. https://maximumfun. org/episodes/sawbones/sawbones-lyme-disease/

[260] Kent, C. 2020. 'Lyme disease: What's actually going on here?' *Pharmaceutical Technology*. Accessed 7 May 2022 from https://www. pharmaceutical-technology.com/features/lyme-disease-whats-actually-going-on-here/

[261] Feder Jr H M, Johnson B J, O'Connell S, et al. 2007. 'A critical appraisal of "chronic Lyme disease"' *New England Journal of Medicine*. 357 (14): 1422-30.

[262] Wormser, G. P and Shapiro, E D. 2009. 'Implications of gender in chronic Lyme disease' *Journal of women's health*. 18 (6): 831–834.

[263] Hamilton, A. 2020. 'Fake it off: Reddit's r/ Illnessfakers community and the politics of disbelief' *Bitch Media*. Accessed 3 March 2022 from https://www.bitchmedia.org/article/ illness-fakers-subreddit-politics-of-disbelief

[264] Fischer, M. 2019. 'What Happens When Lyme Disease Becomes an Identity?' *The Cut*. Accessed 3 March 2022 from https://www. thecut.com/2019/07/what-happens-when-lyme-disease-becomes-an-identity.html

[265] Yunus M B. 2001. 'The role of gender in fibromyalgia syndrome' *Curr Rheumatol Rep*. 3 (2): 128-34.

[266] Goldhill, O. 2018. 'AI can spot the pain from a disease some doctors still think is fake' *Quartz*. Accessed 7 May 2022 from https:// qz.com/1349854/ai-can-spot-the-pain-from-a-disease-some-doctors-still-think-is-fake/

267 Campbell, L. 2021. 'Navigating Hospital Visits When You Have Endometriosis' *Healthline*. Accessed 21 May 2022 from https://www.healthline.com/health/endometriosis/navigating-hospital-visits

268 The President and Fellows of Harvard College. 2021. 'The power of the placebo effect' *Harvard Health Publishing*. Accessed 25 June 2022 from https://www.health.harvard.edu/mental-health/the-power-of-the-placebo-effect

269 Heianza, Y, Ma, W, Li, X, et al. 2020. 'Duration and life-stage of antibiotic use and risks of all-cause and cause-specific mortality: prospective cohort study' *Circulation research*. 126 (3): 364-373

270 Butler T. 2017. 'The Jarisch-Herxheimer Reaction After Antibiotic Treatment of Spirochetal Infections: A Review of Recent Cases and Our Understanding of Pathogenesis' *The American journal of tropical medicine and hygiene*. 96 (1): 46–52.

271 Viegas, J. 2007. 'Laxatives kept Pharaohs on the throne' *ABC Science*. Accessed 26 June 2022 from https://www.abc.net.au/science/articles/2007/03/01/1860103.htm

272 McElroy, S and McElroy, J. 2018. 'Jilly Juice' *Sawbones: A Marital Tour of Misguided Medicine* Podcast Maximum Fun. https://maximumfun.org/episodes/sawbones/sawbones-jilly-juice/

273 Hogg, P. 2021. 'The top 10 medical advances in history' *Proclinical*. Accessed 30 May 2023 from https://www.proclinical.com/blogs/2021-6/the-top-10-medical-advances-in-history

274 Proctor R N. 2006. '"Everyone knew but no one had proof": tobacco industry use of medical

history expertise in US courts, 1990-2002'. *Tobacco control*, 15 (Suppl 4): iv117–iv125.

275 Murray, P. 1996. *The Widening Circle: A Lyme Disease Pioneer Tells Her Story*. New York, NY: St. Martin's Press.

276 Mora, C, Tittensor, D P, Adl, S, et al. 2011. 'How many species are there on Earth and in the ocean?' *PLoS biology*. 9 (8).

277 Summer, J and Rehman, A. 2023. 'Why Do You Yawn?' *Sleep Foundation*. Accessed 30 May 2023 from https://www.sleepfoundation.org/sleep-faqs/why-do-you-yawn

278 NCSE. 2007. 'Gravity: It's Only a Theory' *Reports of the National Center for Science Education*. 27 (5-6) Accessed 20 May 2022 from https://ncse.ngo/gravity-its-only-theory

279 Encyclopædia Britannica. 2022. 'Uncover the science behind the phenomena of lightning and thunder' *Britannica*. Accessed 20 May 2022 from https://www.britannica.com/video/180139/lightning-thunder

280 Herculano-Houzel, S. 2012. 'The remarkable, yet not extraordinary, human brain as a scaled-up primate brain and its associated cost' *Proceedings of the National Academy of Sciences*. 109 (Supplement 1): 10661-10668.

281 Boyd, R. 2008. 'Do People Only Use 10 Percent of Their Brains?' *Scientific American*. Accessed 30 December 2022 from https://www.scientificamerican.com/article/do-people-only-use-10-percent-of-their-brains/

282 Burgess, L. 2018. 'What percentage of our brain do we use?' *Medical News Today*. Accessed 30 December 2022 from https://www.

medicalnewstoday.com/articles/321060

[283] Stafford, T. 2014. 'Can you live a normal life with half a brain?' *BBC Future.* Accessed 30 December 2022 from https://www.bbc.com/future/article/20141216-can-you-live-with-half-a-brain

[284] Kwon, D. 2015. 'What Makes Our Brains Special?' *Scientific American.* Accessed 30 December 2022 from https://www.scientificamerican.com/article/what-makes-our-brains-special/

[285] Ralton, G. 2022. 'Study reveals how human brains have evolved to be smarter than other animals' *Imperial College London.* Accessed 30 December 2022 from https://www.imperial.ac.uk/news/239331/study-reveals-human-brains-have-evolved/

[286] Cobb, M. 2020. 'Why your brain is not a computer' *The Guardian.* Accessed 30 December 2022 from https://www.theguardian.com/science/2020/feb/27/why-your-brain-is-not-a-computer-neuroscience-neural-networks-consciousness

[287] Resnick, B. 2017. 'Brain activity is too complicated for humans to decipher. Machines can decode it for us.' *Vox.* Accessed 30 December 2022 from https://www.vox.com/science-and-health/2016/12/29/13967966/machine-learning-neuroscience

[288] Cox, D. 2017. 'The curse of the people who never feel pain' *BBC Future.* Accessed 30 December 2022 from https://www.bbc.com/future/article/20170426-the-people-who-never-feel-any-pain

[289] Garland E L. 2012. 'Pain processing in the human nervous system: a selective review

of nociceptive and biobehavioral pathways'.
Primary care. 39 (3): 561–571.

290 Zuppinger-Dingley, D, Schmid, B, Petermann, J
S, et al. 2014. 'Selection for niche differentiation
in plant communities increases biodiversity
effects'. *Nature.* 515: 108-111.

291 Blume, H. 1998. 'Neurodiversity' *The Atlantic.*
Accessed 31 December 2022 from https://www.
theatlantic.com/magazine/archive/1998/09/
neurodiversity/305909/

292 Singer, J., 1998. 'Odd people in: The birth of
community amongst people on the autistic
spectrum'. Honours Dissertation. University of
Technology, Sydney.

293 Timberlake, H. 2019. 'Why there is no such
thing as a 'normal' brain' *BBC Future.* Accessed
28 December 2022 from https://www.bbc.com/
future/article/20191008-why-the-normal-brain-
is-just-a-myth

294 Legault, M, Bourdon, J N, and Poirier, P. 2021.
'From neurodiversity to neurodivergence: the
role of epistemic and cognitive marginalization'
Synthese. 199: 12843–12868.

295 Bethel, S. 2021. 'Why you're probably not
neurodivergent' *Stephanie Bethany.* Accessed
28 December 2022 from https://www.
stephaniebethany.com/blog/why-youre-
probably-not-neurodivergent-revisiting-
neurodiversity

296 Crocker, A F, and Smith, S N. 2019. 'Person-first
language: are we practicing what we preach?'
Journal of multidisciplinary healthcare. 12: 125–129.

297 Gernsbacker, M A. 2017. 'Editorial Perspective:
The use of person-first language in scholarly

writing may accentuate stigma' *The Association for Child and Adolescent Mental Health*. 58 (7): 859-861.

[298] Ladd, P. 2003. 'Understanding deaf culture: In search of deafhood' *Multilingual Matters*.

[299] CDC. 2022. 'Signs and Symptoms of Autism Spectrum Disorder' *Centers for Disease Control and Prevention*. Accessed 14 Jan 2022 from https://www.cdc.gov/ncbddd/autism/signs.html

[300] Evans, B. 2013. 'How autism became autism: The radical transformation of a central concept of child development in Britain' *History of the human sciences*. 26 (3): 3–31.

[301] Gewin, V. 2008. 'Autism and Schizophrenia: A tale of two disorders' *Spectrum*. Accessed 14 January 2023 from https://www.spectrumnews.org/news/autism-and-schizophrenia-a-tale-of-two-disorders/

[302] Fischbach, G D. 2007. 'Leo Kanner's 1943 paper on autism' *Spectrum*. Accessed 14 January 2023 from https://www.spectrumnews.org/opinion/viewpoint/leo-kanners-1943-paper-on-autism/

[303] Herman, E. 2019. 'Autism in the DSM' *The Autism History Project*. Accessed 14 Jan 2023 from https://blogs.uoregon.edu/autismhistoryproject/topics/autism-in-the-dsm/

[304] Baron-Cohen, S. 2015. 'Leo Kanner, Hans Asperger, and the discovery of autism' *The Lancet*. 386 (1001): 1329-1330.

[305] Silberman, S. 2015. *Neurotribes: The legacy of autism and the future of neurodiversity*. New York, NY: Penguin.

[306] Hall, A. R. 1980. *Philosophers at War: The Quarrel between Newton and Leibniz*. New York, NY:

Cambridge University Press.

[307] Furfaro, H. 2018. 'New evidence ties Hans Asperger to Nazi eugenics program' *Spectrum*. Accessed 29 December 2022 from https://www.spectrumnews.org/news/new-evidence-ties-hans-asperger-nazi-eugenics-program/

[308] Solomon, A. 2008. 'The Autism Rights Movement' *Andrew Solomon*. Accessed 14 Jan 2023 from http://andrewsolomon.com/articles/the-autism-rights-movement/

[309] Sinclair, J. 1993. 'Don't mourn for us' *Autreat*. Accessed 14 Jan 2022 from https://www.autreat.com/dont_mourn.html

[310] Dekker, M. 2020. 'From exclusion to acceptance: Independent living on the autistic spectrum' *Autistic Community and the Neurodiversity Movement*. Singapore: Palgrave Macmillan. 41-49.

[311] Silberman, S. 2016. 'Autistic people are not failed versions of "normal." They're different, not less' *TED*. Accessed 29 December 2022 from https://ideas.ted.com/autistic-people-are-not-failed-versions-of-normal-theyre-different-not-less/

[312] Silberman, S. 2015. 'Our Neurodiverse World' *Slate*. Accessed 15 January 2023 from https://slate.com/technology/2015/09/the-neurodiversity-movement-autism-is-a-minority-group-neurotribes-excerpt.html

[313] Mell-Taylor, A. 2022. 'We Shouldn't Care If Someone's "Faking" Being Queer For Attention' *Medium*. Accessed 15 January 2023 from https://medium.com/prismnpen/we-shouldnt-care-if-someone-s-faking-being-queer-for-attention-fd4da1d4d627

[314] Burns, K. 2019. 'The rise of anti-trans "radical"

feminists, explained' *Vox*. Accessed 16 January 2023 from https://www.vox.com/identities/2019/9/5/20840101/terfs-radical-feminists-gender-critical

[315] Naraharisetty, R. 2022. 'How Asexual People Feel Excluded From Queer Spaces, Complicating Their Identity' *The Swaddle*. Accessed 16 January 2023 from https://theswaddle.com/how-asexual-people-feel-excluded-from-queer-spaces-complicating-their-identity/

[316] Russell, G. 2020. 'Critiques of the neurodiversity movement' *Autistic community and the neurodiversity movement*. Kapp, S K. (ed). 287.

[317] Jaarsma P and Welin S. 2015. 'Autism, accommodation and treatment: a rejoinder to Chong-Ming Lim's critique' *Bioethics* 29 (9): 684–685.

[318] den Houting, J. 2019. 'Neurodiversity: An insider's perspective' *Autism*, 23 (2): 271–273.

[319] Casanova, M. 2015. 'The Neurodiversity Movement: Lack of Trust' *Cortical Chauvinism*. Accessed 15 January 2023 from https://corticalchauvinism.com/2015/01/05/the-neurodiversity-movement-lack-of-trust/

[320] Reyes, R. 2022. 'Faith' *Faith, Hope, and Love…With Autism*. Accessed 15 January 2023 from https://faithhopeloveautism.blogspot.com/2013/06/faith.html

[321] Villines, Z. 2021. 'Everything to know about nonverbal autism' *Medical News Today*. Accessed 15 January 2023 from https://www.medicalnewstoday.com/articles/non-verbal-autism;

[322] Marcin, A. 2020. 'What It Means If Your 2-Year-

Old Isn't Talking Yet' *Healthline.* Accessed 16 January 2023 from https://www.healthline.com/health/2-year-old-not-talking-but-babbling

[323] Wodka, E L, Mathy, P, and Kalb, L. 2013. 'Predictors of Phrase and Fluent Speech in Children With Autism and Severe Language Delay' *Pediatrics.* 131 (4): e1128–e1134.

[324] Olsson, Regan. 2021. 'TikTok and the Dangers of Self-Diagnosing Mental Health Disorders' *Banner Health.* Accessed 14 May 2022 from https://www.bannerhealth.com/healthcareblog/advise-me/tiktok-self-diagnoses-on-the-rise-why-its-harmful

[325] Australian Institute of Health and Welfare. 2022. 'Mental health' *Australian Institute of Health and Welfare.* Accessed 22 January 2023.

[326] Bashforth, E. 2021. 'Does self-diagnosis work and what are the dangers?' *Patient.info.* Accessed 14 May 2022 from https://patient.info/news-and-features/does-self-diagnosis-work-and-what-are-the-dangers

[327] Bennett, C. 2018. 'The Impact of Self-Diagnosis on the Healthcare Industry' *News Medical Life Sciences.* Accessed 14 May 2022 from https://www.news-medical.net/health/The-Impact-of-Self-Diagnosis-on-the-Healthcare-Industry.aspx

[328] Carr, R. 2011. 'The ups and downs of self-diagnosis' *Healthy Food Guide.* Accessed 14 May 2022 from https://www.healthyfood.com/advice/the-ups-and-downs-of-self-diagnosis/

[329] Baah F O, Teitelman A M, and Riegel B. 2009. 'Marginalization: Conceptualizing patient vulnerabilities in the framework of social determinants of health - An integrative review'.

Nurs Inq. 26 (1): e12268;

330 Cheraghi-Sohi, S, Panagioti, M, Daker-White, G. et al. 2020. 'Patient safety in marginalised groups: a narrative scoping review' *Int J Equity Health.* 19 (26).

331 Baron-Cohen, S, Wheelwright, S, Skinner, R, et al. 2001. 'The Autism-Spectrum Quotient (AQ): Evidence from Asperger syndrome / high-functioning autism, males and females, scientists and mathematicians' *J Autism Dev Disord.* 31 (1): 5-17.

332 Woodbury-Smith, M R, Robinson, J, Wheelwright, S, et al. 2005. 'Screening adults for Asperger syndrome using the AQ: A preliminary study of its diagnostic validity in clinical practice'. *Journal of Autism and Developmental Disorders.* 35 (3): 331-335.

333 Australian Federation of Disability Organisations. 2023. 'Social Model of Disability' *Australian Federation of Disability Organisations.* Accessed 25 February 2023 from https://www.afdo.org.au/social-model-of-disability/

334 Asztély, K, Kopp, S, Gillberg, C, et al. 2019. 'Chronic Pain And Health-Related Quality Of Life In Women With Autism And/Or ADHD: A Prospective Longitudinal Study' *Journal of pain research.* 12: 2925–2932.

335 Haelle, T. 2015. 'Majority Of Autism Increase Due To Diagnostic Changes, Finds New Study' *Forbes.* Accessed 28 December 2022 from https://www.forbes.com/sites/tarahaelle/2015/01/05/majority-of-autism-increase-due-to-diagnostic-changes-finds-new-study/?sh=6f774c5d7c36

336 Davidson M. 2017. 'Vaccination as a cause of

autism-myths and controversies'. *Dialogues in clinical neuroscience*, 19 (4): 403–407.

337 Quick, J D, and Larson, H. 2018. 'The Vaccine-Autism Myth Started 20 Years Ago. Here's Why It Still Endures Today' *Time.* Accessed 27 February 2023 from https://time.com/5175704/andrew-wakefield-vaccine-autism/

338 Alexander, K E. 2020. 'Measles elimination in Australia' *AJGP.* 49 (3): 112-114.

339 Rylaarsdam, L and Guemez-Gamboa, A. 2019. 'Genetic Causes and Modifiers of Autism Spectrum Disorder' *Sec. Cellular Neuropathology.* 13.

340 Baron-Cohen, S. 2018. 'Genetic studies intend to help people with autism, not wipe them out' *New Scientist.* Accessed 16 March 2023 from https://www.newscientist.com/article/2179104-genetic-studies-intend-to-help-people-with-autism-not-wipe-them-out/

341 Autism Speaks. 2016. 'Our Work' *Autism Speaks.* Accessed 19 March 2023 from https://www.autismspeaks.org/autism-speaks-questions-answers-facts#cure

342 Spectrum 10K. 2023. 'Spectrum 10K' *Spectrum 10K.* Accessed 20 March 2023 from https://spectrum10k.org/

343 Sanderson, K. 2021. 'High-profile autism genetics project paused amid backlash' *Nature.* Accessed 20 March 2023 from https://www.nature.com/articles/d41586-021-02602-7

344 Kline, W. 2022. 'How geneticists can gain greater buy-in from the autistic community' *Spectrum.* Accessed 16 March 2023 from https://www.spectrumnews.org/opinion/viewpoint/how-

geneticists-can-gain-greater-buy-in-from-the-autistic-community/

[345] Arizona Board of Regents. 2021. 'Jérôme Lejeune (1926-1994)' *The Embryo Project Encyclopedia*. Accessed 18 March 2023 from https://embryo.asu.edu/pages/jerome-lejeune-19261994

[346] Thomas, G M and Rothman, B K. 2016. 'Keeping the Backdoor to Eugenics Ajar?: Disability and the Future of Prenatal Screening' *AMA Journal of Ethics*. 18 (4): 406-415.

[347] Collins, V R, Muggli, E E, Riley, M, et al. 2008. 'Is Down syndrome a disappearing birth defect?' *The Journal of Pediatrics*. 152 (1): 20-24.

[348] Pain, E. 2014. 'After More Than 50 Years, a Dispute Over Down Syndrome Discovery' *Science.org*. Accessed 18 March 2023 https://www.science.org/content/article/after-more-50-years-dispute-over-down-syndrome-discovery

[349] Bezemer, M L, Blijd-Hoogewys, E M A, and Meek-Heekelaar, M. 2001. 'The Predictive Value of the AQ and the SRS-A in the Diagnosis of ASD in Adults in Clinical Practice' *J Autism Dev Disord*. 51: 2402–2415.

[350] Costandi, M. 2011. 'Simon Baron-Cohen: Theorizing on the mind in autism' *Spectrum*. Accessed 20 March 2023 from https://www.spectrumnews.org/news/profiles/simon-baron-cohen-theorizing-on-the-mind-in-autism/

[351] Lombardo M V, Barnes J L, Wheelwright S J, et al 2007. 'Self-referential cognition and empathy in autism' *PLoS One*. 2 (9): e883.

[352] McGrath, J. 2019. 'Not all autistic people are good at maths and science – despite the stereotypes' *The Conversation*. Accessed 20 March 2023 from

https://theconversation.com/not-all-autistic-people-are-good-at-maths-and-science-despite-the-stereotypes-114128

353 Gernsbacher, M A and Yergeau, M. 2019. 'Empirical Failures of the Claim That Autistic People Lack a Theory of Mind' *Archives of scientific psychology.* 7 (1): 102–118.

354 Doyle, N. 2021. 'Is Everyone a Little Autistic?' *Forbes.* Accessed 28 December 2022 from https://www.forbes.com/sites/drnancydoyle/2021/01/16/is-everyone-a-little-autistic/?sh=43e779645666

355 Hull, L, Mandy, W, Lai, M C. et al. 2019. 'Development and Validation of the Camouflaging Autistic Traits Questionnaire (CAT-Q)' *J Autism Dev Disord.* 49: 819–833.

356 Schuck, R K, Flores, R E, and Fung, L K. 2019. 'Brief Report: Sex/Gender Differences in Symptomology and Camouflaging in Adults with Autism Spectrum Disorder' *J Autism Dev Disord.* 49: 2597–2604.

357 Foley, L. 2020. 'Autism in women: Why it's different and what to look out for' *See Her Thrive.* Accessed 29 January 2023 from https://www.seeherthrive.com/blog/2020/11/5/autism-in-women-why-its-different-and-what-to-look-out-for;

358 Kim, Cynthia. 2013. 'Understanding the gender gap: Autistic women and girls' *Autistic Women & Nonbinary Network.* Accessed 29 January 2023 from https://awnnetwork.org/understanding-the-gender-gap-autistic-women-and-girls/

359 Ratto, A B, Kenworthy, L, Yerys, B E, et al. 2018. 'What About the Girls? Sex-Based Differences in Autistic Traits and Adaptive Skills'. *Journal*

of autism and developmental disorders. 48 (5): 1698–1711.

360 Hull, L, Petrides, K V, and Mandy, W. 2020. 'The Female Autism Phenotype and Camouflaging: a Narrative Review'. *Rev J Autism Dev Disord.* 7: 306–317.

361 Devlin, H. 2018. 'Thousands of autistic girls and women 'going undiagnosed' due to gender bias' *The Guardian.* Accessed 25 February 2023 from https://www.theguardian.com/society/2018/sep/14/thousands-of-autistic-girls-and-women-going-undiagnosed-due-to-gender-bias

362 Szalavitz, M. 2016. 'Autism—It's Different in Girls' *Scientific American.* Accessed 25 February 2023 from https://www.scientificamerican.com/article/autism-it-s-different-in-girls/

363 Baron-Cohen, S, Knickmeyer, R C, and Belmonte, M K. 2005. 'Sex differences in the brain: implications for explaining autism'. *Science.* 310 (5749): 819-823.

364 Guest, K. 2019. 'The Gendered Brain by Gina Rippon review – exposing a myth' *The Guardian.* Accessed 20 March 2023 from https://www.theguardian.com/books/2019/mar/02/the-gendered-brain-by-gina-rippon-review

365 Rippon, G. 2019. *The Gendered Brain: The new neuroscience that shatters the myth of the female brain.* New York, NY: Random House.

366 471 Eliot, L. 2019. 'Neurosexism: the myth that men and women have different brains' *Nature.* Accessed 20 March 2023 from https://www.nature.com/articles/d41586-019-00677-x

367 Costandi, M. 2016. *Neuroplasticity.* Quebec, Canada: MLT Press.

368 Baron-Cohen, S. 2005. 'The Male Condition' *The New York Times*. Accessed 20 March 2023 from https://www.nytimes.com/2005/08/08/opinion/the-male-condition.html

369 Southbank Centre. 2014. 'Fighting the Neurotrash' *WOW 2014*. Accessed 20 March 2023 from https://www.youtube.com/watch?v=2RWvDTKbFHg

370 Baron-Cohen, S. 2010. 'Delusions of gender– 'neurosexism', biology and politics' *The Psychologist*. 23 (11): 904-905.

371 Kim, C. 2013. 'Understanding the gender gap: Autistic women and girls' *Autistic Women & Nonbinary Network*. Accessed 29 January 2023 from https://awnnetwork.org/understanding-the-gender-gap-autistic-women-and-girls/

372 Sacks, O. 2001. 'Henry Cavendish: An early case of Asperger's syndrome?'. *Neurology*. 57 (7): 1347.

373 Goode, E. 2001. 'CASES; A Disorder Far Beyond Eccentricity' *New York Times*. Accessed 29 December 2022 from https://www.nytimes.com/2001/10/09/health/cases-a-disorder-far-beyond-eccentricity.html

374 Yale. 2023. 'Fred Volkmar, MD' *Yale School of Medicine*. Accessed 26 February 2023 from https://medicine.yale.edu/profile/fred-volkmar/

375 Yagoda, M. 2013. 'ADHD is different for women' *The Atlantic*. Accessed 26 February 2023 from https://www.theatlantic.com/health/archive/2013/04/adhd-is-different-for-women/381158/

376 Gunnerson, T. 2022. 'What's the history of ADHD?' *WebMD*. Accessed 28 December 2022 from https://www.webmd.com/add-adhd/adhd-

history

377 American Psychiatric Association. 2022. *Diagnostic and Statistical Manual of Mental Disorders* (5th ed). Washington DC, WA: American Psychiatric Association.

378 Rucklidge J J. 2010. 'Gender differences in attention-deficit/hyperactivity disorder'. *Psychiatr Clin North Am.* 33 (2): 357-73;

379 Hinshaw, S P, Nguyen, P T, O'Grady, S M., et al. 2022. 'Annual Research Review: Attention-deficit/hyperactivity disorder in girls and women: underrepresentation, longitudinal processes, and key directions' *Journal of child psychology and psychiatry, and allied disciplines.* Advance online publication. https://doi.org/10.1111/jcpp.13480;

380 Kinman, T. 2016. 'Gender differences in ADHD symptoms' *Healthline.* Accessed 26 February 2023 from https://www.healthline.com/health/adhd/adhd-symptoms-in-girls-and-boys

381 Hinshaw, S, Littman, E, and Chronis-Tuscano, A. 2023. 'ADHD in Women and Girls: Why Female Symptoms Slip Through Diagnostic Cracks' *Additude.* https://www.additudemag.com/adhd-in-women-girls-symptoms-diagnosis-recommendations/

382 CHADD. 2019. 'Women Often Diagnosed with ADHD Later In Life' *CHADD.* Accessed 26 February 2023 from https://chadd.org/adhd-weekly/women-often-diagnosed-with-adhd-later-in-life/

383 The Chesapeake Center. n.d. 'Gifted/ADHD: High Achievers with ADHD Challenges'

The Chesapeake Center. Accessed 26 February 2023 from https://chesapeakeadd.com/home/education-and-training/articles/gifted-adhd-high-achievers-with-adhd-challenges/

[384] Rabinovici G D, Stephens M L, and Possin K L. 2015. 'Executive dysfunction' *Continuum (Minneap Minn)* 21 (3): 646-59.

[385] Murray, F. 2018. 'Me and Monotropism: A unified theory of autism' *The British Psychological Society*. Accessed 24 September 2023 from https://www.bps.org.uk/psychologist/me-and-monotropism-unified-theory-autism

[386] Ellison, E. 2021. 'Only 10 percent of kids with ADHD grow out of it as adults, research says' *Washington Post* Accessed 26 February 2023 https://www.washingtonpost.com/health/adhd-persists-adulthood-growing-out-study/2021/08/12/68934808-fa03-11eb-8a67-f14cd1d28e47_story.html

[387] Johnson, M. 2012. 'New rules allow joint diagnosis of autism, attention deficit' *Spectrum*. Accessed 29 December 2022 from https://www.spectrumnews.org/news/new-rules-allow-joint-diagnosis-of-autism-attention-deficit/

[388] Hours, C, Recasens C, Baleyte J. 2022. 'ASD and ADHD Comorbidity: What Are We Talking About?' *Frontiers in Psychiatry*. 13.

[389] Rusting, R. 2018. 'Decoding the overlap between autism and ADHD' *Spectrum*. Accessed 29 December 2022 from https://www.spectrumnews.org/features/deep-dive/decoding-overlap-autism-adhd/

[390] Yo Samdy Sam. 2022. '5 signs you have ADHD and autism' *YouTube* Accessed 29 December

2022 from https://www.youtube.com/
watch?v=pMx1DnSn-eg

[391] Leitner, Y. 2014. 'The co-occurrence of autism
and attention deficit hyperactivity disorder
in children – what do we know?' *Frontiers in
Human Neuroscience*. 8: 268.

[392] Marschall, A. 2022. 'What to Know About
Comorbid Autism and ADHD (AuDHD)' *Very
Well Mind*. Accessed 23 April 2023 from https://
www.verywellmind.com/what-to-know-about-
comorbid-autism-and-adhd-6944530

[393] Nielsen, M E, Hammond, A E, & Higgins, L D.
n.d. 'The twice-exceptional project: Identifying
and serving gifted/handicapped learners'
*Context for promise: Noteworthy practices and
innovations in the identification of gifted students*.
Charlottesville: University of Virginia, The
National Research Center on the Gifted and
Talented. 145-168.

[394] Higgins, L D and Nielsen, M E. 2000.
'Responding to the Needs of Twice-Exceptional
Learners: A School District and University's
Collaborative Approach' in *Uniquely Gifted:
Identifying and Meeting the Needs of the Twice-
Exceptional Student*. Gilsum, NH: Avocus
Publishing. 287-303;

[395] Scholnick, J. 2017. 'Giftedness and ADHD: A
strengths-based perspective and approach'
CHADD. Accessed 26 February 2023 from
https://chadd.org/attention-article/giftedness-
adhd-a-strengths-based-perspective-and-
approach/

[396] Corden, K, Brewer, R, and Cage, E. 2021.
'Personal Identity After an Autism Diagnosis:

Relationships With Self-Esteem, Mental Wellbeing, and Diagnostic Timing' *Frontiers in psychology*. 12: 699335.

[397] NIMH. 2023. 'Panic Disorder: When Fear Overwhelms' *National Institute of Mental Health*. Accessed 2 August 2023 from https://www.nimh.nih.gov/health/publications/panic-disorder-when-fear-overwhelms

[398] O'Donoghue, S. 2020. 'How it feels to have an autistic meltdown and how you can help' *BBC Scotland*. Accessed 2 August 2023 from https://www.bbc.co.uk/programmes/articles/38f5MsC2mB5fnmCr5v77zDn/how-it-feels-to-have-an-autistic-meltdown-and-how-you-can-help

[399] NHS. 2023. 'Selective serotonin reuptake inhibitors (SSRIs)' *NHS Inform*. Accessed 24 April 2023 from https://www.nhsinform.scot/tests-and-treatments/medicines-and-medical-aids/types-of-medicine/selective-serotonin-reuptake-inhibitors-ssris

[400] Purves W K, Sadava D, Orians G H, Heller H C. 2001. *Life: The Science of Biology* (6th ed). Sunderland, Massachusetts: Sinauer Associates;

[401] Purves D, Augustine G J, Fitzpatrick D, et al. 2001. *Neuroscience* (2nd ed). Sunderland, Massachusetts: Sinauer Associates.

[402] Modglin, L. 2023. '7 Foods That Could Boost Your Serotonin: The Serotonin Diet' *Healthline*. Accessed 25 April 2023 from https://www.healthline.com/health/healthy-sleep/foods-that-could-boost-your-serotonin

[403] Jenkins, T A, Nguyen, J C, Polglaze, K E. 2016. 'Influence of Tryptophan and Serotonin on

Mood and Cognition with a Possible Role of the Gut-Brain Axis' *Nutrients.* 8 (1): 56.

[404] Randall, A. 2019. 'Mental health: Doctor issues warning over mindfulness apps offering 'quick fix'' *ABC News.* Accessed 23 July 2023 from https://www.abc.net.au/news/2017-05-08/mindfulness-app-ended-up-increasing-my-anxiety/8506438

[405] Ablett, J. n.d. 'How Adrenaline and Endorphins Can Delay the Pain You Feel After a Car Accident' *Pinnacle Health Chiropractic.* Accessed 25 April 2023 from https://www.pinnaclehealthchiro.com/blog/how-adrenaline-and-endorphins-can-delay-the-pain-you-feel-after-a-car-accident

[406] GAAR Law Firm. 2018. 'When Adrenaline Hurts'. *GAAR Law Firm.* Accessed 25 April 2023 from https://www.gaarlaw.com/blog/2018/04/when-adrenaline-hurts

[407] Lieberman, M, Marks, A, and Peet, A. 2013. *Marks' Basic Medical Biochemistry: A Clinical Approach.* Alphen aan den Rijn, Netherlands: Wolters Kluwer Publishing.

[408] Brennan, D. 2021. 'What to Know About an Adrenaline Rush' *Web MD.* Accessed 25 April 2023 from https://www.webmd.com/a-to-z-guides/what-to-know-adrenaline-rush;

[409] Cafasso, J. 2023. 'Adrenaline Rush: Everything You Should Know' *Healthline.* Accessed 25 April 2023 from https://www.healthline.com/health/adrenaline-rush

[410] Sprouse-Blum, A S, Smith, G, Sugai, D. 2010. 'Understanding endorphins and their importance in pain management' *Hawaii medical*

journal. 69 (3): 70–71.

[411] Harvard Medical School. 2021. 'Endorphins: The brain's natural pain reliever' *Harvard Health Publishing.* Accessed 25 April 2023 from https://www.health.harvard.edu/mind-and-mood/endorphins-the-brains-natural-pain-reliever

[412] Juárez Olguín, H, Calderón Guzmán, D, Hernández García, E, et al. 2016. 'The Role of Dopamine and Its Dysfunction as a Consequence of Oxidative Stress' *Oxidative medicine and cellular longevity.*

[413] Pietrangelo, A. 2019. 'How Does Dopamine Affect the Body?' *Healthline.* Accessed 25 April 2023 from https://www.healthline.com/health/dopamine-effects

[414] MacGill, M. 2017. 'What is the link between love and oxytocin?' *Medical News Today.* Accessed 25 April 2023 from https://www.medicalnewstoday.com/articles/275795

[415] Schneiderman, I, Zagoory-Sharon, O, Leckman, JF, et al. 2012. 'Oxytocin during the initial stages of romantic attachment: relations to couples' interactive reciprocity'. *Psychoneuroendocrinology*, 37 (8): 1277–1285.

[416] Uvnäs-Moberg, K, Handlin, L, Petersson, M. 2015. 'Self-soothing behaviors with particular reference to oxytocin release induced by non-noxious sensory stimulation'. *Front Psychol.* 12 (5): 1529.

[417] Lin, T W and Kuo, Y M. 2013. 'Exercise benefits brain function: the monoamine connection'. *Brain Sci.* 11 3 (1): 39-53.

[418] Manninen S, Tuominen L, Dunbar R I, et al. 2017. 'Social Laughter Triggers Endogenous Opioid

Release in Humans'. *J Neurosci.* 37 (25): 6125-6131.

[419] Dunbar R I, Baron R, Frangou A, et al 2012. 'Social laughter is correlated with an elevated pain threshold'. *Proc Biol Sci.* 279 (1731): 1161-7.

[420] Cirino, E. 2018. 'What Are the Benefits of Hugging?' *Healthline.* Accessed 29 July 2023 from https://www.healthline.com/health/hugging-benefits

[421] Mead, M N. 2008. 'Benefits of sunlight: a bright spot for human health'. *Environ Health Perspect.* 116 (4): A160-7.

[422] Perreau-Linck, E, Beauregard, M, Gravel, P, et al. 2007. 'In vivo measurements of brain trapping of C-labelled alpha-methyl-L-tryptophan during acute changes in mood states'. *J Psychiatry Neurosci.* 32 (6): 430-4.

[423] Blood, A J and Zatorre, R J. 2001. 'Intensely pleasurable responses to music correlate with activity in brain regions implicated in reward and emotion'. *Proc Natl Acad Sci U S A.* 98 (20): 11818-23.

[424] Kjaer, T W, Bertelsen, C, Piccini, P, et al. 2002. 'Increased dopamine tone during meditation-induced change of consciousness'. *Brain Res Cogn Brain Res.* 13 (2): 255-9;

[425] Rokade, P. 2011. 'Release of Endomorphin Hormone and Its Effects on Our Body and Moods: A Review' *Semantic Scholar.* Accessed 29 July 2023 from https://www.semanticscholar.org/paper/Release-of-Endomorphin-Hormone-and-Its-Effects-on-A-Rokade/9d6a77f113bb866ea1588edf646a60e25ca1755?p2df

[426] Field, T, Hernandez-Reif, M, Diego, M, et al. 2005. 'Cortisol Decreases And Serotonin

And Dopamine Increase Following Massage Therapy' *International Journal Of Neuroscience.* 115: 10, 1397-1413;

[427] Bolbol-Haghighi, N, Masoumi, S Z, and Kazemi F. 2016. 'Effect of Massage Therapy on Duration of Labour: A Randomized Controlled Trial'. *J Clin Diagn Res.* 10 (4): QC12-5;

[428] Katzman M A, Bilkey T S, Chokka P R, et al. 2017. 'Adult ADHD and comorbid disorders: clinical implications of a dimensional approach'. *BMC Psychiatry.* 17 (1): 302;

[429] Rim, S J, Kwak, K, Park, S. 2023. 'Risk of psychiatric comorbidity with autism spectrum disorder and its association with diagnosis timing using a nationally representative cohort' *Research in Autism Spectrum Disorders.* 104 (102134);

[430] Marno, H E. 2021. 'Is There a Link Between Neurodiversity and Mental Health?' *Psychology Today.* Accessed 29 July 2023 from https://www.psychologytoday.com/au/blog/pathways-progress/202108/is-there-link-between-neurodiversity-and-mental-health

[431] Princing, M. 2022. 'What Is Neurodiversity and Why Does It Matter?' *UW Medicine.* Accessed 29 July 2023 from https://rightasrain.uwmedicine.org/mind/mental-health/neurodiversity-or-neurodivergence

[432] Nao Medical. n.d. 'Neurodivergent Vs Mental Illness: Understanding the Differences and Overcoming Stigma' *Nao Medical.* Accessed 29 July 2023 from https://naomedical.com/info/neurodivergent-vs-mental-illness-understanding-differences.html

[433] Berrall, J. 2022. "Floral decoration' *Encyclopædia Britannica*. Accessed 3 December 2022 from http://www.britannica.com/EBchecked/topic/210629/floral-decoration

[434] Encyclopædia Britannica. 2022. 'Christmas tree' *Encyclopædia Britannica*. Accessed 3 December 2022 from https://www.britannica.com/plant/Christmas-tree

[435] Stott, R. 2016. 'How Flower-Obsessed Victorians Encoded Messages in Bouquets' *Atlas Obscura*. Accessed 3 December 2022 from https://www.atlasobscura.com/articles/how-flowerobsessed-victorians-encoded-messages-in-bouquets

[436] Garber, M. 2021. 'The dark side of the houseplant boom' *The Atlantic*. Accessed 3 December 2022 from https://www.theatlantic.com/culture/archive/2021/04/dark-side-houseplant-boom-nature-empathy/618638/

[437] Hamburg, R. 2015. 'How the space race influenced design' *The National*. Accessed 3 December 2022 from https://www.thenationalnews.com/arts/how-the-space-race-influenced-design-1.55612

[438] Raven, P H, Evert, R F, and Eichhorn, S E. 2005. *Biology of Plants*. (7th ed). New York: W. H. Freeman.

[439] Australian National Botanic Gardens and Centre for Australian National Biodiversity Research. 2012. 'CANBR and ANBG databases' *Information About Australia's Flora*. Accessed 29 July 2023 from https://www.anbg.gov.au/cpbr/databases/

[440] Royal Botanic Garden Sydney. n.d. 'Glossary of Botanical Terms' *New South Wales Flora Online*. Accessed 29 July 2023 from https://

plantnet.rbgsyd.nsw.gov.au/cgi-bin/NSWfl.
pl?page=nswfl&glossary=yes

441 InformedHealth.org. 2006. 'How does the blood
circulatory system work?' *Institute for Quality
and Efficiency in Health Care (IQWiG)*. Accessed 29
July 2023 from https://www.ncbi.nlm.nih.gov/
books/NBK279250/

442 Heifer International. 2018. 'From Sap to Syrup:
How Maple Syrup is Made' *Heifer International*.
Accessed 29 July 2023 from https://www.heifer.
org/blog/how-maple-sugar-is-made.html

443 Murugesu, J A. 2022. 'Antimicrobial drug derived
from tree sap could treat chronic wounds'
New Scientist. Accessed 29 July 2023 from
https://www.newscientist.com/article/2338077-
antimicrobial-drug-derived-from-tree-sap-
could-treat-chronic-wounds/

444 Miller, D. 2018. 'The Difference Between Tree Sap
& Tree Resin' *Sciencing*. Accessed 29 July 2023
from https://sciencing.com/difference-between-
tree-sap-tree-resin-12296179.html

445 Crampton, L. 2022. 'Frankincense, Myrrh, and
Amber: Tree Resin Facts and Uses' *Owlcation*.
Accessed 29 July 2023 from https://owlcation.
com/stem/Frankincense-Myrrh-Amber-and-
Other-Plant-Resins

446 Hortoris. 2020. 'Latex, Opium, Sap, Gum And
Resin' *Gardeners Tips*. Accessed 29 July 2023
from https://gardenerstips.co.uk/blog/articles/
trees-and-shrubs/latex-opium-sap-and-resin/

447 Ho, C C. 2021. 'Fundamentals and recent
applications of natural rubber latex in dipping
technology' *Chemistry, Manufacture, and
Applications of Natural Rubber (2nd ed)*. 317-361.

448 University of Oxford. 2013. 'Plants use latex to harm and heal' *University of Oxford*. Accessed 29 July 2023 from https://www.ox.ac.uk/news/2013-10-30-plants-use-latex-harm-and-heal

449 Carlin, M G, Dean, J R, and Ames, J M. 2020. 'Opium Alkaloids in Harvested and Thermally Processed Poppy Seeds' *Front. Chem.* 8: 737.

450 Norn, S, Kruse, P R, Kruse, E. 2005. 'Opiumsvalmuen og morfin gennem tiderne History of opium poppy and morphine' *Dan Medicinhist Arbog.* 33: 171-84.

451 Santella, T M and Triggle, D J. 2007. *Opium*. Broomall, PA: Chelsea House.

452 Institute of Medicine (US) Committee on Military Nutrition Research. 2001. 'Pharmacology of Caffeine' *Caffeine for the Sustainment of Mental Task Performance: Formulations for Military Operations*. Washington DC: National Academies Press

453 Gorrod, J W and Wahren, J. 1993. *Nicotine and Related Alkaloids*. Berlin, Germany: Springer Dordrecht;

454 Encyclopaedia Britannica. 2023. 'Cocaine' *Britannica*. Accessed 29 July 2023 from https://www.britannica.com/science/cocaine

455 Holesh J E, Aslam S, and Martin A. 2023. 'Physiology, Carbohydrates'. *StatPearls*. Treasure Island, FL: StatPearls Publishing.

456 Lee, A R. 2022. 'Food That's Surprisingly Good (Or Bad) For You. *Columbia University Irving Medical Center*. Accessed 29 July 2023 from https://www.cuimc.columbia.edu/news/food-thats-surprisingly-good-or-bad-you;

457 British Heart Foundation. 2022. 'Why there's

no such thing as 'good' or 'bad' foods' *Heart Matters*. Accessed 29 July 2023 from https://www.bhf.org.uk/informationsupport/heart-matters-magazine/nutrition/good-foods-bad-foods

[458] Marcin, A. 2019. 'How Are Carbohydrates Digested?' *Healthline* Accessed 29 July 2023 from https://www.healthline.com/health/carbohydrate-digestion

[459] Ratan-NM, M. 2019. 'Do Lactase Enzymes Work Against Lactose Intolerance?' *News Medical: Life Sciences*. Accessed 29 July 2023 from https://www.news-medical.net/health/Do-Lactase-Enzymes-Work-for-Lactose-Intolerance.aspx

[460] Graham, D Y, Ketwaroo, G A, Money, M E, et al. 2018. 'Enzyme therapy for functional bowel disease-like post-prandial distress' *J Dig Dis*. 19 (11): 650-656.

[461] Cherney, K. 2021. 'What Are the Different Types of Irritable Bowel Syndrome (IBS)?' *Healthline*. Accessed 29 July 2023 from https://www.healthline.com/health/types-of-ibs#types

[462] NIH. 2023. 'Aloe Vera'. *National Center for Complementary and Integrative Health.* Accessed 29 July 2023 from https://www.nccih.nih.gov/health/aloe-vera

[463] Kytidou, K, Artola, M, Overkleeft, H S, et al. 2020. 'Plant Glycosides and Glycosidases: A Treasure-Trove for Therapeutics' *Front. Plant Sci*. 11: 357.

[464] NIH. n.d. 'Vitamins and Minerals for Older Adults' *National Institute on Aging*. Accessed 29 July 2023 from https://www.nia.nih.gov/health/vitamins-and-minerals-older-adults

[465] Watanabe F, Yabuta Y, Bito T, et al. 2014. 'Vitamin B12-containing plant food sources for

vegetarians'. *Nutrients.* 6 (5): 1861-73.

[466] Wacker M and Holick M F. 2013. 'Sunlight and Vitamin D: A global perspective for health.' *Dermatoendocrinol.* 5 (1): 51-108.

[467] Russell J and Rovere A, eds. 2009. *American Cancer Society Complete Guide to Complementary and Alternative Cancer Therapies.* 2nd ed. Atlanta: American Cancer Society. 116–119.

[468] Baer, H A. 2001. 'The sociopolitical status of U.S. naturopathy at the dawn of the 21st century' *Medical Anthropology Quarterly.* 15 (3): 329–46.

[469] Society of Naturopaths. 2020. 'The History of Naturopathy' *Society of Naturopaths.* Accessed 10 December 2022 from https://societyofnaturopaths.org/about-naturopathy/history-of-naturopathy/

[470] Garrison, F H. 1921. *Greek Medicine. In an introduction to the history of medicine.* Philadelphia, PN: WB Saunders Company

[471] Robinson, J O. 1986. 'Surgical drainage: An historical perspective. *BJS Society.*

[472] Rudiman, R. 2021. 'Advances in gastrointestinal surgical endoscopy' *Annals of Medicine and Surgery.* 72: 103041.

[473] Jouanna, J. 2012. 'Air, Miasma and Contagion in the Time of Hippocrates and the Survival of Miasmas in Post-Hippocratic Medicine (Rufus of Ephesus, Galen and Palladius)' *Greek Medicine from Hippocrates to Galen.* Leiden, The Netherlands: Brill.

[474] Medical News Today. 2018. 'What is modern medicine?' *Medical News Today.* Accessed 29 July 2023 from https://www.medicalnewstoday.com/articles/323538

475 Geffen, L. 2014. 'A brief history of medical education and training in Australia' *The Medical Journal of Australia*. 201 (1): S19-S22.

476 BMJ. 1944. 'The Training of Doctors: Report by the Goodenough Committee' *The British Medical Journal* 2 (4359): 121-23.

477 The Health Foundation. n.d. 'Goodenough Committee report on medical schools' *Policy Navigator*. Accessed 29 July 2023 from https://navigator.health.org.uk/theme/goodenough-committee-report-medical-schools

478 Goodenough, Sir W M. 1944. Report of the inter-departmental committee on medical schools. Richmond, UK: HM Stationery Office.

479 Bamberger, W. 1977. 'Prof. Erwin Mueller, 65; Physicist Was First Person to See an Atom' *The New York Times*. Accessed 29 July 2023 from https://www.nytimes.com/1977/05/18/archives/prof-erwin-mueller-65-physicist-was-first-person-to-see-an-atom.html

480 NASA. 2019. 'July 20, 1969: One Giant Leap For Mankind' *NASA*. Accessed 29 July 2023 from https://www.nasa.gov/mission_pages/apollo/apollo11.html

481 Silver, S. 2018. 'The story of the original iPhone, that nobody thought was possible' *Apple Insider*. Accessed 29 July 2023 from https://appleinsider.com/articles/18/06/29/the-story-of-the-original-iphone-that-nobody-thought-was-possible

482 WHO. 2009. 'Historical perspective on hand hygiene in health care' *WHO Guidelines on Hand Hygiene in Health Care: First Global Patient Safety Challenge Clean Care Is Safer Care*. Geneva: World Health Organization.

[483] WHO. 2018. 'Infant mortality' The global health observatory. Accessed 21 December 2021 from https://www.who.int/data/gho/data/themes/topics/indicator-groups/indicator-group-details/GHO/infant-mortality

[484] WHO. 1980. The declaration of the global eradication of smallpox. *World Health Organization*. https://apps.who.int/iris/handle/10665/155528

[485] AJMC. 2021. 'A Timeline of COVID-19 Developments in 2020' *AJMC*. Accessed 21 December 2021 from https://www.ajmc.com/view/a-timeline-of-covid19-developments-in-2020

[486] Achan J, Talisuna A O, Erhart A, et al. 2011. 'Quinine, an old anti-malarial drug in a modern world: role in the treatment of malaria'. *Malar J.* 10: 144.

[487] Weston, P. 2021. 'Knowledge of medicinal plants at risk as languages die out' *The Guardian*. Accessed 11 December 2022 from https://www.theguardian.com/environment/2021/jun/08/knowledge-of-medicinal-plants-at-risk-as-languages-die-out

[488] Burrowes, K. 2021. 'Gender bias in medicine and medical research is still putting women's health at risk' *The Conversation*. Accessed 11 December 2022 from https://theconversation.com/gender-bias-in-medicine-and-medical-research-is-still-putting-womens-health-at-risk-156495

[489] Care About. 2022. 'The NDIS and fibromyalgia' *Care About*. Accessed 11 December 2022 from https://www.careabout.com.au/ndis/fibromyalgia

490 Veeresham, C. 2012. 'Natural products derived from plants as a source of drugs' *Journal of Advanced Pharmaceutical Technology & Research*. 3 (4): 200–201.

491 Scott J R, Hassett A L, Brummett C M, et al. 2017. 'Caffeine as an opioid analgesic adjuvant in fibromyalgia' *J Pain Res*. 10: 1801-1809.

492 Harte, S, Hassett, A, Brummett, C, et al. 2012. 'Daily caffeine consumption is associated with fibromyalgia pain'. *The Journal of Pain*. 13 (4): S32.

493 Singal, J. 'The Psychological Quirk That Explains Why People Fear Harmless Chemicals' *The Cut*. Accessed 11 December 2022 from https://www.thecut.com/2015/04/psychology-of-scary-sounding-chemicals.html

494 Francl, M M. 2013. 'Curing chemophobia: Don't buy the alternative medicine in 'The Boy With a Thorn in His Joints' *Slate*. Accessed 11 December 2022 from https://slate.com/technology/2013/02/curing-chemophobia-dont-buy-the-alternative-medicine-in-the-boy-with-a-thorn-in-his-joints.html

495 Jackson, C. 1994. 'Ban Dihydrogen Monoxide!' *Coalition to ban DHMO*. Accessed 4 December 2022 from http://www.dhmo.org/facts.html

496 NCCIH. 2022. 'Natural Doesn't Necessarily Mean Safer, or Better' *Natural Center for Complementary and Integrative Health*. Accessed 10 December 2022 from https://www.nccih.nih.gov/health/know-science/natural-doesnt-mean-better

497 Russo, E B. 2011, 'Taming THC: potential cannabis synergy and phytocannabinoid-terpenoid entourage effects'. *British Journal of Pharmacology*, 163: 1344-1364.

498 Proofed. 2023. 'Fallacy Watch: What Is Faulty Generalisation?' *Proofed* Accessed 29 July 2023 from https://getproofed.com.au/writing-tips/fallacy-faulty-generalisation

499 United States Department of Agriculture. 2022. 'The Powerful Solanaceae: Belladonna' US Forest Service. Accessed 10 December 2022 from https://www.fs.usda.gov/wildflowers/ethnobotany/Mind_and_Spirit/belladonna.shtml

Milton Keynes UK
Ingram Content Group UK Ltd.
UKHW041902120324
439302UK00005B/242

9 780645 985221